Gloria Ganger
Bought 2/99
@ Christian Retreat

9/8/99 Started reading

The Song

of

The Bride

The Song
of
The Bride

by Jeanne Guyon

Published by
The SeedSowers
Christian Books Publishing House
P.O. Box 285
Sargent, GA 30275

ISBN 0-940232-38-3

Publisher's Preface

The place is a small town just northeast of Paris, called Meaux. The scene is a large room in a building adjoining the church structure. Though no one is calling it that, a trial is going on. The accused is Jeanne Guyon. The powers in the palace of Versailles have strongly hinted they want a guilty verdict. Archbishop Bossuet is in charge of this "investigation." He is the most powerful churchman in France and, perhaps, in all Europe. He has been called "The Catholic Church's answer to Martin Luther."

Bossuet asks Guyon to submit some of her writings, those best presenting her spiritual views, to the three-man council who stands in judgment of her.

Not realizing the utter unfairness of theologians in such matters as these, she trustingly makes a fatal blunder. She submits her commentary on *The Song of Songs*. Now this book (the most embarrassing book in the Bible) is full of some of the most intimate and explicit language of love that could be found anywhere in the seventeenth century!

Bossuet is a priest. Let us give him the benefit of doubt and assume he has never broken his priestly vows. That means this very self-righteous fellow has never had sex, and we conclude, therefore, that he has little or no firsthand knowledge of such things. He also lives in an age and in a church where the idea of sex is still vaguely associated with sin, no matter who is doing it! He is also about as close to pure intellect as a human being can be. (If we did not count his vast vanity, he would have been very close to 100 percent intellect.) Guyon, in turn, is one of history's great emoters! She has, for instance, without embarrassment, reported moments of sexual delight with her husband so intense she has fainted dead away! This is also the woman who has an almost incomparable internal relationship with her Lord, and she also has written a commentary on *The Song of Songs!*

The woman's fate was sealed, for Bossuet was the first man to read this commentary still in manuscript form! His hair stood on end! As far as he was concerned, the book was not fit for human eyes to see, and its author was stark raving mad. The fallout was that Jeanne Guyon was eventually sent to prison, first in Vincennes, and finally in the infamous Bastille.

With that as background, you will be surprised to learn that both scholars and history have been kind to Guyon's interpretation of *The Song of Songs.* At that time her interpretation of this particular book had never been presented from the view she took. She makes the book personal, a story of love between believer and Lord. All commentaries before had seen the bride either as the church or as Israel. Today many who study this book conclude that not only is Guyon's basic thesis correct, but her interpretation of the book sound. Her insight into *The Song of Songs* has been historically influential.

Here, then, for the first time in modern English, is one of the most controversial (and best) books of the seventeenth century. That this work was written to aid believers in their individual walk with Christ, and that it came from the incomparable heart of this passionate French woman . . . is sufficient enough to commend the book to us.

The Editors

Publisher's Note

Several people have cooperated in rewriting this book into easily readable modern American English. It was a difficult task because the Bible that Jeanne Guyon, writing in the seventeenth century, had available to her was an ancient Catholic translation. We used her version, as it was, as much as we found it feasible to do so. In some cases we wove in some phrases from a standard version.

As for Jeanne Guyon's commentary on the Song, if we have changed the language too much for the few who loved our former old-English version, we apologize. We tried very hard to say what Guyon said, but in an easily readable language. We are sure this modernized version will be more helpful to more readers.

Footnotes are placed at the end of each chapter.

Author's Introduction

There are some who say that deep union with God cannot happen in this life. I am confident, however, that your spirit can deeply touch and be united with God's spirit while you live in the body. Of course, this union is experienced but not actually seen in the physical realm. There, when you fully enter the presence of God, you shall fully see all that you now touch by faith.

The moment you receive Christ you receive all you need to live and enjoy the Christian life. Christ within you is the fullness of God. What I am suggesting in this commentary is not an experience that you need to have. No I am explaining that your spiritual life is a journey toward Christ possessing you more completely.

You can receive and enjoy Christ without seeing Him face to face. In the night of faith you have the pleasure of enjoyment but without the satisfaction of physical sight. When you stand before Him you will have the clear vision of God in addition to the happiness of being His. But your temporary blindness does not stop your true enjoyment of God nor the real communication of His Word to your spirit. This experience does not come from a flight of fancy; the richness of deep and lasting union with God will be testified to by all who have experienced it.[1]

Initial surrender to Jesus Christ comes long before you totally surrender to Him and know Him in His fullness. There is no doubt that when you first receive Him you are united to Him, but there is much work that He must do in you to make you perfectly fitted for Himself. This fitting process takes a long time and must occur before God can fully communicate Himself to you.

All this is more real than can be expressed. In fact, your goal is to allow God to possess you without holding anything back from Him. True union with God is permanent and lasting because it is inward and spiritual.[2] Complete union with God is your final destination. Your spirit can be poured into Him. He is your center. In Him your spirit can be transformed. God, in creating you, made you a partaker of Himself. He made you to be reunited with Him, and He gives you an inner urge toward that reunion.

On a human level, God gives man the desire to be fully united with a spouse in marriage; but that union is never totally complete because the two can never totally merge into one. This is like trying to melt two very different kinds of metals together. They can never be totally united because of their different properties. The more alike the two metals are, the more readily they mix. On the other hand, if you mix two glasses of water together, they immediately become so fully mixed that you cannot separate them.

Your spirit is perfectly made to be united and transformed into God. You truly are made to be married to Him. There may be an initial union with God without this deeper merging of your spirit with His. But this deep exchange is the kind of union with God that I am discussing. Your spirit can be united to God in this way because that is what it is made for. Paul called this "being changed into the same image" (II Corinthians 3: 18). Jesus called it "oneness" (John 17: 11, 21–22).

Deep union with God takes place only when you surrender your self-nature to exist only in God. There is a deep fellowship where you stop preserving the self, and lovingly and perfectly sink into God. Certainly this does not mean that you lose your own personality and become God.

If you allow a drop of water to fall into a cup of wine, the water loses its own form and character. The water is apparently changed into wine; however, the water will always remain distinct in some way. So you see that you will never become God, and you do have the choice to separate yourself from Him.

Deep and lasting union with God, the spiritual marriage, is what you should ask of your Beloved. Let your passion cause you to proclaim to Him your deepest desire: "Let Him kiss me with the kisses of His mouth." The bride in *The Song of Songs* asks it of Him as though she were addressing someone else; in third person: an impetuous exclamation of love, giving vent to her passion without specifying to whom she is speaking. She says that only a deep union can satisfy her, and that is what she demands.

The Author
(Edited)

Notes To Introduction

1. We will enjoy perfection in the world to come, which, of course is different from the spiritual life we can have here; but let us not, for that reason, make our experience sadly imperfect by depriving it of its essential spiritual elements. Even here in this world, our union with Christ in the spirit is the greatest achievement of God's love and omnipotence. As John of the Cross has written, the work of our regeneration and salvation is more stupendous than that of our creation. - *Justifications,* by Jeanne Guyon.

2. There is never a moment in which God does not shed His infinite love of benevolence upon every human being; for being communicable in his nature, He must necessarily communicate Himself incessantly to every being disposed to receive His gifts, as the dew falls upon every object exposed to the sky. But man is created free, and has the power of shutting himself up, and of sheltering himself from the celestial dew; he turns his back upon God and heaps hindrance upon hindrance, lest he should be reached by His mercy. When he removes some of the obstacles he had put in the way, he is induced to turn towards the Lord who unceasingly rains love upon every heart. No sooner is the heart turned and opened a little, than the dew of grace falls gently into it, and according as it is more or less abundant, so is the growth of love in the heart; the more widely the soul is opened to God, the more profuse is the fall of the dew.

   But it is to be remembered that Love prepares His own way; no other can do it for Him; He prepares our heart and leads it from fullness to fullness; He enlarges, and as He enlarges, fills; for He abhors an empty heart, and though He seems at times to reduce souls to emptiness and nakedness, the desolation is only external and apparent. It is true that He thrusts out everything that is not God; for as God is Love, He can permit only Himself in the soul; all else is offensive to Him. He therefore sets every engine in motion, that He may purify his follower, enlarge, extend and magnify him, in order that He may have room enough to dwell in.

But O, holy Love! Where, ah! where are the hearts that will submit to be thus purified, enlarged, and extended by Thy hand? Thine operations only seem harsh because we are impure, for Thou art always gentle and tender-hearted! We must even esteem it a great matter, if some souls will give Thee a hesitating admission. Alas! How restricted art Thou in such hearts! What confined quarters and what a filthy residence for the infinite God of purity! O Love! Hast Thou not the power of God? Must we make no other use of our liberty but in resisting Thee? Sad gift—the only true employment of which is in sacrificing it wholly to Thee?—*Justifications.*

1

CHAPTER 1:1—*Let him kiss me with the kisses of his mouth.*

What is this kiss? It is complete spiritual union: a real, permanent, and lasting experience of God's nature. The kiss is the union of God's spirit to your spirit.

When a person is first converted, he is united to God but he has not yet come to experience Him deeply. There is a deep and abiding union with Christ that you can come to know. The height and breadth and depth of God will take an eternity to know. Here is what this woman, the bride of Christ, cries out to know.

There are two kinds of union with God. One is to feel a sense of His presence for a few moments or hours. Deep and lasting union, however, continues in the midst of any circumstance. Let me try to explain. When you first come to experience the Lord you do not know Him very well. There is much in you that is not like Him and you do not understand the purpose of your Lord. This time is like an engagement period. God stirs up your love for Him, you present each other with tokens of your mutual affection, but you still do not fully know or enjoy your Beloved.

But there is a deeper union with God that can be thought of in terms of a spiritual marriage. Your spirit is fully united to Him. You are His without reservation. There is a communication of substance: God unites Himself with your spirit, and you are able to begin to explore the fullness of God.

The journey toward this complete union is what is being described in the *Song of Songs:* It is a place where your spirit is completely possessed by God. Barrenness and unfruitfulness are not known here. The "kiss of His mouth" is nothing less than the vital communication of the Word of God to you.

Consider that God is called "the Word." His touch to the spirit is the perfect enjoyment and consummation of spiritual union. God communicates Himself, and His Word, to your spirit.

CHAPTER 1:1,2—*For your love is better than wine and your ointments more fragrant than the choicest perfumes.*

God's nourishment, especially at the beginning of the spiritual life, is sweet and pleasant. The strongest men who drink wine are not as strong as those who receive His strength and nourishment.

The bosom of God is so fragrant with sweet perfume that it draws you to receive from Him happily and gratefully. Resting in His bosom is like a precious oil that heals every inward wound. Since this is true, what delight shall there be in the kiss of His mouth?

The *Songs of Songs* begins with an announcement of what is to come. The *Song* tells what the Bridegroom will be rewarded with (His beloved bride), and how perfect that reward is. It is, of course, natural to think of the happy wedding day during the engagement. As there are many steps needed to prepare for a marriage, so it is with the spiritual marriage. The journey has many trials and much work that must be endured before you can receive the kiss of His mouth. Therefore, the *Song of Songs* begins with a view toward final union. This is what causes His bride to ask, even from the beginning, for the kiss of His mouth. This kiss, however, is the final thing that she will receive.

CHAPTER 1:2—*Your name is as oil poured forth; therefore have the virgins loved you.* 9/16/99

Grace which can be experienced—here signified by the name of the Bridegroom—powerfully penetrates the spirit. God pours out His grace on those that He intends to fill with His love. His name is truly a healing balm poured forth. The name of the Bridegroom is so lovely that you find yourself wholly overcome by His power and sweetness. Love takes place without any force. Your spirit is so full of love, and you find the love of your Beloved so pleasurable, that you allow yourself to be carried away by the innocent and wonderful charms of love.

This is how God causes young hearts to love Him. When you are first drawn to God you love Him because of the pleasure that love brings.

It was this oil of gladness with which the Father anointed the Son, placing Him above all others who shall share His Father's glory with Him.

CHAPTER 1:3—*Draw me, we will run after you to the fragrance of your perfume.*

The young maiden asks to be drawn to her Bridegroom from deep within her spirit. She is not satisfied to experience Him only in the physical senses. The bride already understands that there is an enjoyment of her Bridegroom deeper and more lasting than what she now knows. This causes her to make a new request. "Draw me," she says, "into the most inward parts of my spirit, so that I might completely run to You. I will run after You by turning toward You deep within my spirit. There You are—already drawing me toward You! Let me be guided by Your fragrance. I have already been attracted by the perfume which You have poured out on me. It is healing all the evil that sin has caused me. Such wonderful ointment has also purified me from the corruption within me. Allow me to even outrun your fragrance to reach You, the center of my joy."

4

This excellent perfume causes you to desire inward prayer. It will cause you to run after the fragrance of your Lord in order to taste with delight how good He is.

CHAPTER 1:3—*The King has brought me into his chambers; we will rejoice and be glad in you. We will remember your love more than wine; the upright love you.*

No sooner have you revealed your desire to pass by everyone in order to run to Him, than He calls you into His chambers. He is rewarding you for a love that is already somewhat pure. Here is greater grace than what you have known before, but it is still not the ultimate union that you will come to know.

When your heart displays enough faithfulness to be willing to give up the gifts of God in order to reach God Himself, God will shower you with the very gifts that you have set aside. But God quickly removes Himself from those who are only seeking His gifts and graces, and not Him alone.

The Psalmist understood such a thought when he urged all men "to seek the Lord and His strength; to seek His face evermore" (Psalm 105:4). He warns you to not stop at following God for what He can give you. The gifts of God are only the rays that shine forth from His face. So rise up to His throne and seek Him. Seek His face until you are so blessed as to find it.

Now His bride is filled with unspeakable joy for she knows that she is found in Him. She prefers the Bridegroom over everything else. Here is the height of her joy and pleasure. The maiden has already chosen the sweetness of God's milk before the wine of the pleasures of the world. God is more important to her than all of the spiritual comforts that He offers.

She adds another thought: "The upright love You." True uprightness leads you to leave all the pleasures of earth and all the enjoyments of heaven to be lost in God alone. Here is pure and perfect love. For none but the upright can love God as He deserves to be loved!

CHAPTER 1:4—*I am black, but lovely, daughters of Jerusalem, as the tents of Kedar, as the curtains of Solomon.*

The greatest experience of the grace of God will produce in you a deeper knowledge of what you are. Such grace would not come from Him if it did not give you a clear view of your miserable state apart from God. As you come out of the chambers of your king you discover that you are black. What makes you black? Suddenly you see all your faults by the light of God. Until now you had not been aware of your blackness. Now you see that you have not yet been cleansed from yourself.

You see both your faults and your beauty for you

6

say, "I am black but lovely." For you to experience your inner condition is extremely pleasing to your Bridegroom. You beg Him to visit you in a place of rest. Because you have no voluntary sin, you are beautiful to Him. The Bridegroom makes you fair with His own beauty. The blacker you are in your own eyes, the fairer you become in His.

The curtains of Solomon represent your humanity which conceals the Word of God made flesh within you. He has caused you to partake of His beauty; He has concealed His divinity in your humanity. The outer blackness hides God's inner workings within.

You are black from the trials and persecutions which attack you from all sides; yet you are as beautiful as the curtains of Solomon because the cross makes you like your Beloved. Outward weakness appears in you, but your intention is pure within.

CHAPTER 1:5—*Look not upon me because I am dark. The sun has tanned me. My mother's children were angry with me; they made me a keeper in the vineyards; but my own vineyard I have not kept.*

You are now entering into a place of faith that will hide the sense of God's presence that makes it so easy for you to do good. No longer will you easily be able to perform "good works" because God is requiring something else of you. To others it seems that you have fallen back into your old nature.

① P. 20

7

So appears the evidence to the eyes of those who do not see as God does. Although you outwardly appear black, you beg your companions to see beyond that to what God is doing within you. Your outward faults, real or apparent, do not exist because you lack love and courage. Your flaws are seen because the divine Light has looked upon you with His burning face, and this has changed your color: He has taken away your natural way in order to have only what His fiery strength wants to give you. Here is violent love that dries up and tans the skin! Love has not left you, but grown more fierce.[2]

This blackness is progress, not failure. But do not try to imitate such blackness. Only He can produce this color. For His glory, and for His bride's highest good, He burns up and destroys your dazzling outward complexion.

Outward beauty can blind others to your true state. You may even be greatly admired by others and still the Bridegroom's glory not be fully revealed in you because others are too taken up with your outward appearance and acts.

People urge you to resume your active life. They direct your attention to the outward rather than toward the destruction of your inwardly wayward passions. The "mother's children" strive against you for awhile, and you are not able to resist them. You begin to attend to outward and external things. You do not "keep your own vineyard," which is your inward spirit where God lives. This, however, is the only thing that you should keep, and the only

8

vineyard that you should tend. Slowly you become inattentive to the voice of God. You are even less faithful in guarding the inward lives of others. Like the experience of this maiden, you may find that others will be angry with you for turning to find your Lord. Others may see your inner life causing you to neglect outer things. Do not forget to seek your Lord within. You need not be concerned with correcting your external faults. The Bridegroom is well aware of your flaws and will heal them in His own wise way.

CHAPTER 1:6—*Tell me, you who my soul loves, where you feed your flock, where you rest at midday; for why shall I begin to wander after the flocks of your companions?*

You will, sooner or later, be forced to leave your inward retirement, the place of your inward rest, to tend to outward matters of lower description. The more your desire to retire is thwarted, the more your heart becomes inflamed toward your Beloved. You beg him to show you where He feeds His flocks; you want to eat the food that He gives those that are under His care.

When Jesus was on earth, His food and drink was to do the will of the Father (John 4:34). Now His food is to see His friends do His Father's will. His bride feeds upon Him. In Him you find the most lovely and eternal perfection which causes you to

9

love Him more. The more the Shepherd reveals Himself, the more His flock seeks to love Him.

Where does He rest at noon? You ask this so that you might learn the nature of eternal love from its Author. You do not want to wander into a human path, under some guise of false spirituality, and be misled by self-love.

This mistake is common among the flocks of God. Sometimes people are guided by leaders who are not dead to the things of this world, and who do not teach their followers to deny themselves so that Christ might live in them. If you follow a human path you will turn aside from the true Way. You may jump from one spiritual guide to another and frequently change your beliefs without ever arriving at anything solid.

This wandering arises from a failure to listen to the sweet and clear voice of Jesus Christ. Look to Him to give what He alone can give. Only He can keep His flock from going astray.

Do not let yourself be stopped by human plans, no matter how religious. God alone can teach you to do His will, for He alone is God (Ps. 143:10).[3]

Ask the Word of God to bring you to the Father. He—the Word—is the way that leads to the Father. The bosom of the Father is where He rests at noon in all His glory. Desire to be lost in God with Jesus, His Son. There is where you will want to rest forever. In His bosom you will be perfectly safe. Sin cannot deceive you there, and He will keep you from wandering away.

CHAPTER 1:7—*If you do not know, fairest among women, go out by the footsteps of the flock, and feed your young goats beside the shepherd's tent.*

The Bridegroom replies to His bride, and prepares her to receive His grace. He gives a most important instruction: "If you do not know . . . go forth." He suggests that you cannot know the one you love except you also come to know yourself as you really are. You may passionately seek to know your God, but you must also see your *nothingness* next to His *everything*.

But how will you see this? The light needed to discover your nothingness exists only in seeing the all of God. He directs you, therefore, to "go forth." Where? From yourself. How? Through letting go of yourself. You must allow no natural satisfaction in yourself or in any other person. To where? To enter into God by an absolute self-surrender where you will find that He is all and in all (Colossians 1:17; 3:2). You need to see yourself, and everyone else, as nothing in the light of God.

"Nothing" does not deserve praise, for it is nothing. If you hope to experience abiding union with God, you must be persuaded of your own nothingness in light of God's all. You must learn to come out of yourself with deep mistrust of your own abilities. Reserve everything you are for God alone. In this way you will be prepared for lasting union with God.

Learn to leave your self-nature by continually

11

giving up every selfish interest. The Bridegroom prescribes this inward work for those who desire to know Him deeply. He calls you to "go forth" toward an inward course of faith.

The Bridegroom desires that you also not neglect your duties in the place where He has called you. You must follow the Holy Spirit's leading in all the freedom of the inward life. You must also conform to some semblance of the external trappings of faith by being obedient to proper authority. To "go forth" in the footsteps of the flock is to go forth in the common, ordinary way.

CHAPTER 1:8—*I have compared you, my love, to my company of horsemen in Pharoah's chariots.*

10/14/99

The Bridegroom knows perfectly well that all the compliments He lavishes upon you, far from making you vain, only deepen your death to self. He praises you so that your love may grow.

He desires a course so swift and sure for you that you can only be compared to a whole company of riders running toward Him at full speed. Yet while you are on earth He has hidden you by causing you to look like the chariots of Pharoah. You who run so swiftly after him often appear to be on an erratic course. Others may believe that you are in search of the pleasures and vanities of Egypt. Perhaps they will believe that you are eagerly seeking after your own selfish desires. The truth is that you are running toward God, and your race shall end in God

12

alone. Nothing shall stand in the way of your safe arrival. God will supply you with His strength and faithfulness. T. Y.

10/19/99

CHAPTER 1:9—*Your cheeks are lovely as a turtledove's; your neck as jewels.*

The cheeks represent both the inner and the outer life. Here they are compared to the beauty of a turtledove. The dove marries for life. If the dove's partner dies, the dove remains single without seeking another mate.

If you were ever separated from your God, you could find no pleasure in anyone or anything else. If your Bridegroom is known within, you will not try to occupy yourself with other distractions. No lasting enjoyment can be gained from outward pleasures. Your separation from every person and practice that is not of God makes you beautiful in the eyes of your Lord.

The neck represents pure love. For though the neck lacks adornment, the beauty of your complete love and trust is enough. Even without jewels, the bride's completely unbridled love for her Beloved makes her most beautiful.

CHAPTER 1:10—*We will make you gold chains inlaid with silver.*

Already beautiful in your simple, pure heart and

unfeigned love, you shall be given something to add to your beauty—gold chains—to represent your perfect submission to the will of the King of Glory. These chains represent pure love which has one purpose: to do everything for God's pleasure and glory. Nevertheless, the chains will be inlaid with silver. This signifies that no matter how wonderful pure love is, love must still be made visible in good works.

Note carefully that your Divine Master has taken special care in these passages to instruct you toward the supreme purity that He requires in His beloved. He expects you to neglect nothing, in His service or in the service of others.

11/11/99

CHAPTER 1:11—*While the King was resting on his couch, my perfume sent forth its fragrance.*

You experience a sense of the deep and central presence of the Bridegroom. The Bridegroom is ever in the center of your spirit. He dwells there, however, in such a hidden way that you are sometimes unaware of His presence. At certain times the Bridegroom reveals Himself to you and you sense Him deeply and intimately within your spirit.

As you are totally given to Him, you can indeed call him "King." He reigns over you and guides you completely. As an earthly king rests on his couch, so the Eternal King rests in the midst of your spirit.

The perfume, your faithfulness, sends forth a fragrance that is sweet and pleasant. The king is happy to reveal himself to you. You recognize that He rests within you on His royal couch. Although He always abides there, you will not always perceive Him within you.

11/12/99

CHAPTER 1:12—*A bundle of myrrh is my well-beloved to me; he shall abide between my breasts.*

When the bride finds her Groom she is so overcome with joy that she is eager to be immediately united with Him. But this is not yet to be. He is like a "bundle of myrrh" to His beloved.

He is not yet a Bridegroom to be lovingly embraced, but a bundle of trials, pain, and tribulation. He is the crucified One who desires to test your faithfulness to Him by causing you to partake of a good share of His suffering.

Note, however, how far His Bride has progressed: She does not say that her Well-Beloved will give her a bundle of trials and tests. He, Himself, is the bundle. All that she bears, He bears. This bundle of myrrh shall be placed close to her heart as an evidence that He will be a Bridegroom of bitterness both inwardly and outwardly.

External trials are a small matter if they are not accompanied by inward ones. Inward trials are all the more painful, however, if they are accompanied by external problems. The spirit perceives nothing but the cross on every side; nevertheless, here is the

15

Well-Beloved coming to you in the shape of the cross. He is never more present to you than in those seasons of bitterness when He dwells deeply in your spirit.

12/27/99

CHAPTER 1:13—*My Beloved is unto me as a cluster of cypress, in the vineyards of Engedi.*

You do not yet know the depths of the blessedness and beauty of your Beloved. He will dwell wholly in you, and you in Him. Already, though, you are discovering His nearness to be like a "cluster of cypress" (a fragrant shrub). He is the One who gives fragrance and value to everything that is done by those who seek Him.

The maiden compares her Well-Beloved to the pleasant fragrance and excellent properties of balsam. He is the true drink—the strength of the wine of God. As you learn to find your joy in God alone, you can no longer delight in anything else. To seek any other source of satisfaction is to lose quickly all that is from Him.

12/28/99

CHAPTER 1:14—*Behold, you are fair, my love; behold you are fair; you have doves' eyes.*

The Beloved, seeing your readiness to be taught by Him, is charmed with your beauty. He compliments and praises you. The Lord sees in you two kinds of beauty—one outward, the other inward.

Now He wants you to see your beauty also: "Behold, you are already fair within, even though you are not yet perfect. Know, too, that soon you will be perfectly beautiful without. I will perfect you and draw you out of your weakness."

Such praise is accompanied by the promise of a greater beauty. Christ encourages you to find strength in knowing that all your present imperfections establish humility within you; yet He will perfect you so that you will be entirely without blemish. You already have "doves' eyes"—you are simple within and without: Within, you do not turn away from beholding your King; without, your words and actions are free from deception.

Simplicity is the surest sign of spiritual progress. You will learn that you can use no artificial means to reach your Beloved. Let His Spirit lead you. Love is perfected in simplicity and honesty.

12/29/99

CHAPTER 1:15—*Behold, you are fair, my beloved, and lovely; our bed is adorned with flowers.*

The maiden, seeing that her Bridegroom has deeply praised her, is unwilling to spend this praise on herself. She heaps it all back on Him. "Behold, You are fair, my Beloved, and altogether beautiful." She gives back to Him all the praise she has received.

Always try to surpass your Beloved in lavishing praise. He is the worthy One—the Author and Center of all good. Nothing belongs to you. Let the

17

maiden teach you this, as she does so well. Everywhere and always she gives glory to her Lord for everything He is. If she is beautiful, it is with His beauty.

"Our bed," she adds, (which is that inner place where He dwells within), is ready and adorned with the flowers of a thousand virtues. She calls it "our bed" because it is there that the Bridegroom will be encouraged to come and be fully united with her. This was her first request, and this will be her final end.

CHAPTER 1:16—*The beams of our house are of cedar, and our rafters are of cypress.*

The Lord, hidden in the deepest part of your spirit, enjoys pouring out His presence from His dwelling place within you. These outpourings produce much spiritual fruit. The fruit blossoms abundantly like flowers. You are pleased to find yourself in such a wonderful place.

Perhaps, however, you feel that your inward dwelling place is nearing completion. The roof is on; the rafters are of cedar. These beams represent the practice of outward virtues. Good works give off a pleasant fragrance, and at this point you find them easy to practice. Control of your outward nature seems as strong as the beautifully carved rafters of cypress.

Everything appears complete to you because your

bed is adorned with flowers and there is much sweetness within. This causes you to believe that all is in order. Remember, however, what cypress represents: death. All of this beautifully decorated wood is but fuel for the coming sacrifice. Soon you will be but a lily of the valley—a flower of death and suffering.

Notes To Chapter One

P. 7

1. While the believer still feels the full power of the divine unction upon him, his imperfections appear to be destroyed; but as the work of purification goes on, the virtues sink deep into the soul, disappearing from the surface, and leaving the natural defects in conspicuous prominence.

   The effects of winter upon the vegetable world seem to me to present a lively and truthful image of this operation of God. As the season of cold and storms approaches, the trees gradually lose their leaves, their vivid green is soon changed into a funereal brown and they fall and die. The trees now look stripped and desolate; the loss of their summer garments brings to light all the irregularities and defects in their surfaces which had previously been hidden from view. Not that they have contracted any new deformity; not at all; every thing was there before, but hidden by their abundant verdure. Thus the man in the time of his purification, appears stripped of his virtues; but as the tree, in the preservation of its sap, retains that which is the producing cause of leaves, so the soul is not deprived of the essence of virtue, nor of any solid advantage; but only of a certain external facility in the display of its possessions. The man, thus spoiled and naked, appears in his own eyes and in the eyes of others with all the defects of nature which were previously concealed by the verdure of obvious grace.

   During the whole of winter, the trees appear dead; they are not so in reality, but, on the contrary, are submitting to a process which preserves and strengthens them. For what is the effect of winter? It contracts their exterior, so that the sap is not uselessly expended abroad, and it concentrates their strength upon the root, so that new roots are pushed out and the old ones strengthened and nourished and forced deeper into the soil. We may say then that however dead the tree may appear in its accidents (if we may be allowed to apply this expression to its leaves), it was never more alive in its essentials, and it is even during winter that the source and principle of its life is more firmly established. During the other seasons it employs the whole force of its sap in adorning and beautifying itself at the expense of its roots.

Just so in the economy of Grace. God takes away that which is accidental in virtue, that he may strengthen the principle of the virtues. These are still practiced by the soul, though in an exceedingly hidden way; and in humility, pure love, absolute abandonment, contempt of protecting the self and sometimes others, the soul makes solid progress. It is thus that the operation of God seems to sully the soul exteriorly; in point of fact it implies no new defects in the soul, but only an uncovering of the old ones, so that by being openly exposed they may be better healed.—*Justifications,* by Jeanne Guyon.

2. Just as fire blackens wood before consuming it, it is the approach of the fire that blackens the wood, and not its removal. Wood may also be discolored by moisture; but it is then far less fit to be burned, and may even be made so wet that it will not burn at all. Such is the blackness of those who depart from Thee, O God, and go whoring from Thee. (Psalm 73:27.) They shall all perish; but not so our spouse, who is rendered dark-complexioned by the excess of the love that intends to perfect her in Himself, by cleansing her of everything opposed to His own purity.—*Justifications.*

3. A father has caused various dishes to be placed upon the table, some far more delicious than others. One of the children has taken a fancy to the dish that stands nearest him, though it is far from the best, and requests to be helped from it because of his liking for it. The father perceives that if he were to give him a far better one he would reject it, his mind being set upon that which he sees before him; and so, lest he should remain hungry and discouraged, He reluctantly grants him his request.—Thus God granted the prayer of the Israelites for a king; it was not what He would have chosen for them, nor what they needed, but it was what their hearts were set upon having.—*Ascent of Carmel,* by John of the Cross.

21

2

CHAPTER 2:1—*I am the flower of the field and the lily of the valleys.*

You must see that you are first called to rest upon the painful bed of the cross before you can truly rest upon a flowery couch which is *within* you. You have become a flower of death. The most severe death must take place in those in whom He will take root. To find Him you will have to engage in combat and endure many hardships.

CHAPTER 2:2—*As the lily among thorns, so is my love among the daughters.*

By these words the Groom tells of the progress of His beloved. You are like a pure and pleasant lily and a sweet fragrance before Him. There are other daughters, however, who are not yet pliable and submitted to His Spirit. They are like a deep, impenetrable thicket of thorns. Anyone who tries to approach these thorns is wounded. Such people are self-possessed and still taken up with their own will. When you desire to completely yield to the will of God, others who are not so yielded may do everything they can to turn you away from total consecration to God. Treatment like this causes you great suffering. The lily, however, perfectly preserves its purity and its perfume, even when surrounded by thorns. Those who are abandoned to the will of God are kept by the Bridegroom despite all opposition which they experience from those who prefer to be their own guides and to do their own works, without following the moving of God's grace.

1/3/08

CHAPTER 2:3—*As an appletree among the trees of the wood, so is my beloved among the sons. I sat down under the shadow of him whom I desired, and his fruit was sweet to my taste.*

What a simple comparison! The persecuted maiden speaks to those who do not understand her experience and to her Beloved at the same time. The Beloved is the most pleasing sight in heaven and in earth. So do not be surprised that His bride sits under the shadow of His protection. Where else would she want to be? His fruit, even the fruit of the cross, is sweet to taste. This fruit is not sweet to the flesh, but to the spirit. Once tasted, it is more desirable than anything else.

CHAPTER 2:4—*He brought me into the wine-cellars and set love in order within me.*

You come from your delightful fellowship with the King intoxicated with love. No wonder, for you have tasted of the finest wine. You are overtaken by your intense love for your Beloved. The King has brought you into His wine-cellars where you will drink deeply of Him.

The first time you experienced the strength of this excellent wine it overcame you to such a degree that you almost would have preferred milk. The King was content, therefore, to offer you only a small drink so that you might experience who He is. Now that experience and grace have caused you to grow stronger and wiser, you drink freely of the wine of God. He causes you to wholly forget yourself and delight in Him alone. You let go of every selfish interest in your own salvation, perfection, joy, and comfort. Now the only things that interest you are the things that interest God.

No longer do you selfishly think of enjoying His embrace; you are ready to bear His sufferings with Him. You ask nothing for yourself: All is for Him. Fully embrace the righteous plans of your God. Agree, with your whole heart, to all that He chooses for you. Love no one, not even yourself, except that you love them in God. No matter how important or necessary something appears, do not do it unless you act in and through God.

Such is the love that God sets in order within you. The love within you is single-minded and is set on God alone. Everything else is counted as nothing. All is for the Beloved and nothing is for yourself.

What strength does this well-ordered, single-hearted love give for the hard times that are to follow! Love like this can be enjoyed only by those who have tasted it.

CHAPTER 2:5—*Sustain me with flowers, refresh me with apples; for I am lovesick.*

As soon as the Bridegroom sets His love within you, then He gives you a special grace for the sufferings which are to come. He blesses you with fellowship deep within your spirit. The sense of His presence pervades your whole being. An outpouring of divine grace overcomes you. You cry out to be strengthened with little external practices of faith. Is the inward path too much for you?

Poor child! What are you saying? Why talk of being comforted by flowers and fruits—mere external comforts? You do not know what you ask for! If you faint under this trial, you will only fall into the arms of your Love! Wouldn't that be a happy way to die? But you are not yet ready for this.

CHAPTER 2:6—*His left hand is under my head, and his right hand shall embrace me.*

You begin to understand the mystery of what is happening in you. You repent of the outward support you had looked for. The hand of your Lord is enough support. He upholds you with great care. He has honored you with union with Himself. What business do you have with flowers and fruits—that is, with things of the earth—since He favors you with things divine. You are going to be united with Him and that union shall produce fruit incomparably more beautiful than anything you have ever seen. He will embrace you with His right hand, which is His almighty strength and love. Here is perfect enjoyment.

At first, the embrace of the right hand is a sign of an engagement, not a marriage. By the Spirit He will bind you to Himself in an engagement. Now you have the genuine hope of a future marriage. In that day He will so embrace you and unite you with Himself that you will never fear separation.

As your spirit is more deeply united with the Spirit of the Lord, you are strengthened. You are able to bear more and more of God's Presence without growing faint. Confirmed in love, you live in God. "Whoever dwells in God dwells in love; for God is love" (I John 4:16).

1/04/00

CHAPTER 2:7—*I charge you, daughters of Jerusalem, by the gazelles, and by the does of the field, that you do not stir up or awaken my love until she pleases.*

You sleep in a spiritual sleep in your Betrothed's arms. You enjoy a holy rest that you have never known before. Previously you rested under His shadow in confidence, but you have never slept on His bosom or in His arms. How strange a thing that people, even spiritual people, are eager to awaken you from this gentle slumber.[1]

The daughters of Jerusalem are loving but meddlesome souls. They are anxious to wake you for apparently the most valid reasons. But you are so soundly asleep that you cannot be awakened. The Bridegroom speaks for you, holding you in His arms and charging others not to awaken His dear one. He tells the impetuous daughters that you are more pleasing to Him at rest than in most outward activity. "Do not wake her," He says, "nor disturb her sleep. When I am ready to call her, she will be pleased to awaken and follow."

CHAPTER 2:8—*The voice of my beloved! Behold, he comes, leaping upon the mountains, skipping upon the hills.*

Your spirit, asleep to everything else, is all the more attentive to the voice of God. You hear and recognize His voice at once. The Bridegroom both embraces you and dwells within you. He surrounds you and He indwells you. In your spiritual rest you feel that He is uniting Himself more deeply to you. He does not merely walk upon the hills (which are the more external parts of your soul), but upon the mountains (the deepest part of your spirit). You perceive that your experience is far deeper and much different from merely sensing God: You are in union with God. This union will deeply change you within, but it is still not the end of your journey.

28

CHAPTER 2:9—*My beloved is like a gazelle or a young stag; behold, he stands behind our wall; he looks through the window and gazes through the lattice.*

When you receive the sweet touch of the Bridegroom, you think that it will last forever. But if this touch is a pledge of His love, it is also a token of His departure. Just when you begin to taste the sweetness of union with Him, He totally disappears.

The maiden compares His sudden disappearance to the movements of a deer or gazelle. While she is fondly lamenting His strange abandonment, she suddenly senses Him close at hand. He had only hidden Himself to test her faith and confidence in Him. He never removed his gaze from her, but protected her more carefully than ever.

The Bridegroom is more closely united to you than ever before. Although He always sees you, you do not always see Him. You do sense Him occasionally, so that you are not unaware of His watchfulness and so that you may share Him with others.

Notice that He stands. It is no time to rest, nor even to be seated. Now is the time to run.

CHAPTER 2:10—*Behold, my beloved speaks to me and says, "Rise up, my love, my dove, my fair one, and come."*

God turns you within, toward Him, and prepares

you for union with Him through His holy embrace. He does this by causing you to take a road that looks like spiritual death. The Beloved speaks to you and invites you to come quickly out of yourself. He no longer asks you to rest, but commands you to rise up.

This is very different from His former actions. Before, He forbade anyone to wake you. Now He, too, wants you to rise up. He calls you so sweetly and strongly that even if you had not been entirely convinced to do His will, you could no longer resist.

"Rise up, my love, whom I have chosen as my bride. You are my fair one. I find you lovely for you reflect my character. Rise up, my simple and faithful dove, and come forth, for you have everything needed to leave yourself behind. I have led you deeply within to find Me; now I come out and ask you to follow Me out of yourself."

This is not the same kind of "coming forth" that was asked of you before. The first was a call to leave natural gratifications in order to please your Beloved. Here is a call to depart from your self-nature. You must lose possession of yourself in order to be possessed by God alone. Lose sight of yourself—see God alone.

CHAPTER 2:11—*For lo! the winter is past, the rain is over and gone.*

There are two winters: one inner and one outer. These winters occur in opposite seasons. When it is

30

winter without, it is summer within, so you are willing to turn more deeply within: You are drawn to a season of inwardness.

Likewise, when it is winter within, it is summer without. Now a season of cold within causes you to come out of yourself. You are enlarged by an abundant grace of abandonment and thus make more room for your Beloved to live in.

The winter spoken of here is an outward one. This winter is past; you could have frozen from the excessive cold or been overwhelmed by the snows and storms of sins and imperfections that do come so easily while we are occupied in the outward human things. You, however, become strong during the time when you have experienced the Lord within while the storms were raging without. You will no longer fear the raging storms.

The expression, "the winter is past," also suggests that winter brings death to everything. Death has come to all outward things. External pleasures no longer satisfy you. Of course, you may enjoy innocent pleasures, but you enjoy them with a simplicity and detachment that you did not have before. To find any real pleasure in the external things of the world is impossible without the most extreme rebellion.

The winter rains are over and gone. You may go out without fear of the weather. And you have this additional advantage: The cold has destroyed all the insects—that is, things that were formerly active in you and would have destroyed you.

31

CHAPTER 2:12—*The flowers have appeared on the earth: the pruning-time is come, and the voice of the turtledove is heard in our land.*

To persuade you to come forth, He helps you to understand that He is going to lead you into His territory. He calls it "our land" because He has won it for you by His redemption. The land belongs to Him; it also belongs to you through Him. Flowers appear there. The flowers that grow there never fade, for they have no fear of winter coming again.

The time for pruning the vine has come. You, like the vine, must now be pruned, cut down, and stripped.

The voice of the turtledove—the humanity of Christ—invites you to lose yourself and hide yourself with Him in the bosom of the Father. Christ calls you to a land which you, as of yet, do not know. You will understand it better when you have entered into the place He calls you to (the land). For now, though, His voice of simplicity and innocence is different from yours.

CHAPTER 2:13—*The figtree has put forth her green figs, and the flowering vines give a pleasant fragrance. Arise my love, my fair one, and come.*

Eternal spring, accompanied by the fruits of autumn and the heat of summer, is here. The Bridegroom points out three distinct seasons by these fruits and flowers. He no longer refers to winter, for winter has come and gone—both the outward winter and the inward winter.

Here is a season that is made of spring, summer, and fall joined together. Before reaching the inner winter, you passed through all the seasons of the spiritual life. After this, however, you re-enter a perpetual spring-summer-autumn, immortalized by the death of winter. The mildness of spring does not prevent the fervor of summer or the fruitfulness of autumn. The heat of summer does not interrupt the beauty of spring. The fruits of autumn put up no obstacles to the enjoyment of spring nor to the lush growth of summer.

Blessed land! Happy are the ones who possess you!

Come out of yourself to enter this land! He who owns the land promises the land to all. The purchase was made with His blood, even after He had already inherited it; and He earnestly invites all to enter into it. The Bridegroom furnishes you with all the means of doing so. He draws you with urgent invitations. Why do you not quickly enter in?

CHAPTER 2:14—*My dove, in the clefts of the rock, in the hollow of the wall, show me your face and let your voice sound in my ears; for your voice is sweet, and your face is lovely.*

You are hidden in His wounds. These wounds are clefts in the Living Rock. The Bridegroom asks to

33

see your face. Why would He ask this if you were turned completely toward Him? Why does He beg you for a sight of your face? You are hidden in Him—does He not see you? He wants to hear your voice; and you are interested in no one but Him. Once you thought you must always turn inward to find your Bridegroom. So you try to do this again with all your strength. But just the opposite is needed. The Bridegroom is calling you out of yourself.

For this reason He says, "Show me your face, let your voice sound in my ears. Turn toward me, for I have moved to a new place." He assures you that your voice is calm, sweet, and peaceful. In this way you are like your Beloved. His voice is not loud; neither is yours. Your face is beautiful, reflecting His. Your spirit is already fair and beautiful. The only thing you need to do is to "come forth." Why is this so hard?

If He did not so sweetly, yet so forcibly, draw you out of yourself, you would never leave yourself. Now you feel yourself drawn outward with as much force as you formerly felt to retire within—perhaps even more. More power is needed to draw you out of yourself than for you to sink down within yourself.

You remember how wonderful it was to retire within yourself and fellowship there with your Beloved. How hard it is to leave this inward enjoyment and find nothing but trials! In retiring, you live and possess yourself. But when you come out of yourself, your old nature begins to die.

34

CHAPTER 2:15—*Take us the little foxes that spoil the vines; for our vine is in blossom.*

Ask, as this woman does, for your Beloved to take away the little foxes (the many little defects within you). These defects spoil the inward vine which blossoms in your spirit. Yet the Lord is allowing the little foxes to spoil the inner sense of His presence. How else will you be able to abandon your selfish attachment to this wonderful vine of sweet communion?

The Master Himself permits the little foxes to spoil the vine and play havoc with it! If He didn't do this, you would never come out of yourself, for you are so in love with yourself and also, at this point, with the enjoyment you have in your inner fellowship with your Lord. You are reluctant to have Him call you out to another place.

CHAPTER 2:16—*My beloved is mine and I am his; he feeds among the lilies.*

There is unimaginable happiness for you as you wholly and unreservedly devote yourself to your Lord. Your Beloved is everything. You are overcome by His goodness. As the Bridegroom calls you to leave yourself, you believe that you have reached the height of all happiness and the summit of all perfection. You may even believe that you are entering complete union with God.

You know that you belong to your Beloved: He

may do with you what pleases Him. He feeds among the lilies of your purity. He feeds upon His very own life within you. He lives upon innocence and purity, nourishing you with this same food. He invites you to eat with Him the food which He likes best. (Isa. 55:2)

2/14/00

CHAPTER 2:17—*Until the day breaks and the shadows flee away, turn my beloved, and be like a gazelle or a young stag upon the mountains of Bether.*

You sense that you no longer perceive the Word of God within you. You believe that He is sleeping in His place of rest. You say to Him, "My Beloved, since I am under the same roof with You, turn a little toward me so that I may sense You! Let me enjoy the delights of your company until the day breaks, when you will be more visible to me. Let me feel your presence until the shadows of faith yield to the soft light of vision and unclouded enjoyment."

Remembering the first wonderful union which you experienced with Him you cry, "Run quickly if it seems good to You, but let it be on the mountains. Let me enjoy the deep union that was so sweet and profitable when it was given to me before."

Note to Chapter Two

1. Those who are beginning to serve God are commonly persecuted by the unregenerate because their withdrawal is a public condemnation of the disorders which reign in the world. Not so, however, with those who devote themselves to the interior life; not only do they suffer persecution at the hands of a godless world and from people of regular lives, but far more severely from such pious and spiritual-minded persons as are not interior. These latter do it as a matter of duty, not being able to recognize any other way as right but that in which they themselves are walking. But their most violent assaults come from pretended saints and false devotees, whose foul characters, wickedness and hypocrisies they detect as they are enlightened by the truth of God. This gives rise to an opposition between such persons and those who are truly spiritual, like that between the angels and the devils.—*Justifications,* by Jeanne Guyon.

3

2/13/00

CHAPTER 3:1—*By night on my bed I sought him whom my soul loves; I sought him, but did not find him.*

To your dismay you discover that the Bridegroom does not grant you the favor that you have counted on. Before He had given you more than you had ever hoped for; now you are discouraged at His long absence. It is time to seek Him inwardly during the night of faith. Nowhere, however, can you find Him! Still, you continue to seek Him inwardly: This is where He revealed Himself to you and gave you the deepest revelation of His character.

Dear bride! Can you find Him nowhere? Do you not know that He wants you to seek Him no longer within *you,* but within *Himself?* You certainly will not find Him anywhere outside of Himself.[1] Leave yourself quickly so you will find yourself only in Him! *In Him* is where He wants you to be! What a wonderful plan the Bridegroom has! When He is most drawn to you, He flees from you with the greatest cruelty. Here is love's cruelty! For without such cruel love you would never leave yourself. And you could never know what it is like to be lost in God.

2/15/00

CHAPTER 3:2—*I will rise now and go about the streets of the city. In the highways I will seek him whom I love. I sought him but did not find him.*

Here is a miracle performed by the absence of God! How often He invited you to rise up from your rest and you could not do it! He asked you so tenderly, but you were so full of the peace and tranquility which you enjoyed that you could not be persuaded to leave yourself.

The rest you enjoyed in yourself is but a shadow of the rest you will find in God. But it was impossible to convince you of this. Since you no longer find your Beloved in your resting place, you are persuaded to look for Him. The couch which was once a paradise is now a hell, for your Beloved is gone. If He were there with you, hell would be paradise.

The city, which is the world you have hated, will be where you now look for Him. You are not fully instructed, no matter how much love you feel. The bride, who longs to possess the Bridegroom, still speaks as a child. You are so weak that you cannot, at first, seek God in Himself. When you do not find Him within you, you look for Him everywhere else: in a thousand places where He is not.

As you look in vain you may become occupied with the world while you use the excuse that you are

40

looking for your Beloved. Still you look for Him. Your spirit loves Him and can find no rest but in Him. Of course you do not find Him because God has not left you to be found in other people. He wishes you to seek Him in Himself. When you find Him in Himself you will discover a great truth. The beauty of this truth will overwhelm you: The Beloved is everywhere and in everything. He is in all places without being trapped in any of them. His creation is not equal to Him, but He is able to be found everywhere.

2/17/00

CHAPTER 3:3—*The watchmen that patrol the city found me and I asked, "Have you seen my beloved?"*

Since you have not found your Beloved in any mortal person, you seek Him among those who guard His city. The watchmen find you because they are always looking out for His city. These watchmen (Isaiah 62:6), whom God has set upon the walls of Jerusalem, never hold their peace day or night. You ask them for news of your Beloved, but they cannot tell you where He is. Mary Magdalene, when she does not find Christ in the tomb, seeks Him everywhere. Likewise, you search for your Beloved, but no one can tell you where He is but He Himself.

2/18/00

CHAPTER 3:4—*It was soon after I passed by the watchmen when I found Him whom I love. I held him and would not let him go until I brought him into my mother's house and into the room where she conceived me.*

Having come forth from yourself, you leave everything behind to find Him. The Beloved shows Himself to you in new ways. This causes you to believe that you are about to enter a deep and permanent union with God. You cry out in joy, "I have found Him whom my soul loves. I will hold Him and never let Him go." You foolishly think that you can hold onto Him. You believe He left you only because of some fault that you had committed. Now you feel that you will hold Him so tightly, and will give yourself to Him with such faithfulness, that you will never let Him go. You will bring Him "into your mother's house"—that is, into the bosom of God, where you were born and brought forth.

What kind of foolish talk is this, dear woman? It is His right alone to take you. You have no right to lead Him! Love believes everything is possible. Mary believed she could carry away the body of the Lord (John 20:15). The deep desire you feel to be with Him causes you to forget that you must be there with Him and clothed with Him. You foolishly think that you will lead Him.

2/19/00

CHAPTER 3:5—*I charge you, daughters of Jerusalem, by the gazelles and the does of the field, that you do not stir up nor awake my love until she pleases.*

42

The Bridegroom is full of compassion for His bride. He sees the pain of your first deep inward trial since you rose up. Once again He communicates His love to you. You are so overcome with the possession of a treasure which seems even greater than before, that you fall asleep and expire in the arms of Love. The Beloved allows you to sleep. He keeps you from being awakened because it would hinder your death to self and spoil your happiness.

You may suffer greatly in your search for your Beloved, but the pain of that search is but a shadow in comparison with the joy that will come from finding Him. Paul says the same thing when he tells you that the greatest sufferings of life are not worthy to be compared with the glory that shall be revealed in us (Romans 8:8).

2/20/00

CHAPTER 3:6—*Who is she that goes up by the wilderness, like a pillar of smoke, from the incense of myrrh, and frankincense, and all the powders of the perfumer?*

The friends of the Bride, seeing that you are filled with grace from the visit of your Bridegroom, express their astonishment. You become so pure in the arms of your Beloved that you seem like a breath of air consumed by the fire of love. Your uprightness is like smoke rising. Your spiritual nature is clearly evident.

Smoke rising has interesting characteristics. Smoke arises from something that was once solid.

43

Because the solid object has been burned up, smoke flows forth. You are no longer solid and self-contained. You flow upward, coming forth from the wilderness of faith. Where are you going? To rest in God.

2/21/00

CHAPTER 3:7—*Behold his bed, which is Solomon's; sixty valiant men surround it, the valiant ones of Israel.*

The bride, already feeling separated from herself, thinks that there is but one thing more to be done. This is true, but what obstacles must first be overcome!

To reach the bed of the true Solomon, which is God, you must pass through sixty brave soldiers. These soldiers are the characteristics of God's nature. In them you will find all your strength. By these attributes the power of God is revealed to men.

2/22/00

CHAPTER 3:8—*They all hold swords, being expert in war; every man has his sword on his thigh because of fear in the night.*

These soldiers will do battle with anyone who is foolish enough to attribute to self that which belongs to God. They shout in unison, "Who is like unto God?" The righteousness of God comes to fight and destroy the self-righteousness of man. His strength brings to nothing the power of man.

44

The Lord causes you to enter, through an experience of your own infinite weakness, into the strength of the Lord (Psalm 71:16). You learn to dismiss all thoughts of your own righteousness and see that God alone is righteous.

God's providence brings to nothing human foresight and fleshly planning. All this must be destroyed before you are admitted into Solomon's bed. These soldiers, who carry the Word of God like a sword, search deeply within you to find out your secret presumptions; and they are aptly fitted to destroy them.

The Word reveals Himself deep within you so that He may accomplish all that He speaks. No sooner does He declare His word than, like a stroke of lightning, He does it. He reduces all that opposes Him to ashes. When Christ was on earth it was the same way. He spoke and it was done. He took on human form in order to confound the pride of man.

Christ entered into your weakness in order to destroy its strength. He took the form of a sinner so He could stamp out self-righteousness. Your Lord does the same within you. He humbles, abases, and weakens you so that you might see your inability to live without Him.

This passage tells you that the valiant ones are armed for "fear of the night." The nature of God fights against all that keeps you in darkness. He fights against your self-nature which takes for itself all that rightfully belongs to God.

CHAPTER 3:9—*King Solomon made himself a chariot of the wood of Lebanon.*

The Son of God made Himself a chariot of His humanity. The King of Glory confined Himself to human form. He revealed Himself when He became flesh. Within Him, the nature of God and the unfallen nature of man became one for all eternity. The eternal God became mobile as a man. He descended from the wood of Lebanon: from the patriarchs, prophets, and kings known for their good character.

The Word of God also dwells in you, the believer. He sits on the throne of His majesty (II Cor. 5:19), reconciling the world to Himself. Christ constructs a throne for Himself in every person. He adorns this throne in great splendor so that He might reign there. He bought this place within you with His blood. By His grace this throne is made holy. Let Him reign there as king. God reigns in Jesus Christ in the same way that Christ reigns in pure hearts. He looks for those who offer Him no resistance and who have nothing in them that offends Him. With such people He will build His kingdom and make them to share in His royal state, for His Father has appointed Him a kingdom and shared His glory with Him.

The throne of the King of Kings is made of the wood of Lebanon. The foundation of the spiritual building is the redeemed humanity of mankind. This is represented here by the trees of Lebanon.

The bride is an example of the reign of Christ. As a member of the bride of Christ you display your perfect submission to the Heavenly Bridegroom. Each member encourages the others to pursue the eternal happiness of submission to Christ. The Bride herself describes His throne further:

2/24/00

CHAPTER 3:10—*He made the pillars of silver and the couch of gold. The ascent is of purple and the middle of it is decorated with love for the daughters of Jerusalem.*

The pillars of the humanity of Jesus Christ are of silver. He is revealed in the most refined and brilliant silver. His couch, which is the divine nature of Christ, is made of gold. The ascent, or the entry way, speaks of the journey of Jesus Christ. Although He always dwelled in the bosom of the Father, He voluntarily submitted to becoming man. And He could not go back to the Father and enter His glory except through his passion and the shedding of His blood.

The middle of the royal chariot is decorated with gold ornaments: This shows that love is the crowning glory of all the fruits of the Spirit. Jesus Christ contains all the treasures of wisdom and knowledge in the fullness of the Godhead bodily (Col. 2:3,9). Christ was given the Holy Spirit without measure. The Holy Spirit fills the middle of the majestic throne of God. Through the Holy Spirit, God extends His love to you: He binds pure spirits to Christ. This is the love which the Divine Solomon bestows upon His elect daughters of Jerusalem.

The sanctuary God prepares for Himself in His beloved is framed with pillars of silver (which are the gifts of the Holy Spirit). His gifts shine like silver and provide the material for the foundation of the throne.

The couch is of gold. You are called to be as a royal couch for Christ to rest upon. Such a high calling demands no other foundation than God Himself. Every other support will be emptied out of you.

Through much tribulation you enter the Kingdom of God (Acts 14:22). You must suffer with Christ in order to reign with Him (II Tim. 2:12). Tribulation and suffering will be yours if you are to experience, in this life, deep union with the heavenly Bridegroom. The amount of trials, reproaches, and death you will suffer will be beyond what you now imagine.

Last, the middle is covered with love. The throne of God is adorned and decorated with all the fruits and ornaments of love: the fruit of the Spirit and every good work.

See your calling, daughters of Jerusalem! See what the King of Kings wants to give you if you will but give Him your love! Mutual praise is the foundation that the Bridegroom and His bride build upon.

2/24/00

CHAPTER 3:11—*Go forth, daughters of Zion, and behold King Solomon with the crown which his*

48

*mother crowned him with in the day of his wedding,
and in the day of the gladness of his heart.*

Christ invites all inward believers, who are
daughters of Zion, to come out of themselves. Behold your King with the crown of glory given to
Him by God Himself! He is clothed in His divine
conquests, and He desires to share them with you.

Note to Chapter Three

1. Those who have had little experience may object here, that since it is necessary after all to come forth out of self in order to seek the Lord in Himself, it would be a more reasonable direction to bid the beginner seek Him in that way in the first place, instead of sending him the round-about way of first seeking Him within and then without. But this would be a great mistake; for such a one looks for Him as for something quite distinct and separate; he even searches heaven for Him.

In this way, instead of becoming interior and collecting all the forces of his spirit, as David did, to call upon God, his strength is dissipated and wasted. We see the slender and scattered lines of a drawing mutually approaching and strengthening each other as they near the central point, but becoming feeble and indistinct in proportion as they recede from there. So the strength of the believer's spirit, the more it is concentrated within, increases in its ability to function appropriately. And as these lines, however widely separated, are united in the point of view, so the functions of the believer's spirit are diverse and distinct when at a distance from the center. Once assembled deep within, though, they constitute but a single undivided, though not indivisible point, and are endowed with singular power of seeking their Lord.

In order to become interior and spiritual, then, we must begin by seeking the Lord within; but, when once arrived there, we must depart again, not by returning towards the external multiplicity, the point whence we set out, but by passing through beyond self in order to reach the Lord. This going forth from self is not effected by the way by which we entered in, but, as it were, by a way leading through one's self and beyond, from the believer's center to the center of the Creator.

The believer's spirit may be regarded, in short, as a sort of halfway house or inn, by which the traveler must necessarily pass, but, in leaving which, he is not obliged to

50

retrace his steps, but passes onward still by the high road. And as the way to the inn is longer in proportion as we were previously dissipated and removed from our center, so the further we pass it, the further do we leave self behind, both in sight and feeling. No sooner are we arrived at our inmost being than we find our Lord there and are invited, as I have said, to come forth again from ourselves and pass onward; and then we very really pass into Him; for it is there that He is truly found—where our self is no longer. The further we journey, the further we advance in Him, and the further we depart from ourselves.

Then our progress in God should be measured by our separation from self; that is, as to our views, feelings, remembrances, self-interest and self-reflections. While the Christian is advancing towards his center, he is wholly absorbed in self-reflection, and the nearer he comes, the more intense is his absorption, though in more simplicity. When, however, he has arrived there, he ceases to behold himself, just as we see everything about us, but not what is in us. But in proportion as he passes away from and beyond himself, he sees less and less of self because his face is turned the other way, and he cannot look back. Hence those self-reflections which were useful in the beginning become exceedingly injurious at the last. At first, our views must be self-directed and complex; they then become simple and incomplex, without ceasing to have a selfish direction; and then the soul is gifted with a single eye. As the traveler, approaching the inn, which is in full view, has no need of consideration, but fixes his eye steadily upon it, but having entered it, no longer beholds it; so the believer, arrived at his center, may be said to behold self no longer, though in fact he has a mode of perception appropriate to his state. When, however, he has passed beyond self, he no longer feels nor perceives self, but the further he advances in Christ, the less does he discover himself, until at last wholly lost in the abyss of the Lord, he no longer feels, knows, nor discerns anything but Him. Then it is plain that all reflections are hurtful and mortal, for they turn the

Christian into the way that leads from God, and would bring him back to self.

Now this passing beyond self is accomplished by means of the surrender of the will, which, as sovereign of the powers, carries with it the understanding and the memory, which though separate and very diverse powers, are yet one and indivisible in their center. Now, I say, and it is clear, that this state is attended with a sort of stability; and the more it advances the firmer it grows; for it is evident that he who has passed beyond and left self is an entirely different person in his functions from him who is yet striving to reach self and his center; and if the former should endeavor to enter again the latter road, he would find it difficult if not impossible.

So then, we see that they who have reached self and passed beyond, must ever put a greater distance between them and self, and they who desire to be tranformed must continually endeavor to poise themselves in their spirit. To compel a man who has already entered into Christ to resume the way and the practices by which he reached his position would be like endeavoring to force the food which has been digested and passed into the intestines to return by the mouth, a result which only arrives as the sequel of horrible pains and the forerunner of death. While the food remains in the stomach, however, it may be discharged by vomiting, just as we, while still continuing in self, may return upon our ways with greater or less ease, according as we are more or less advanced towards the center of our being; but afterward, to fall back to our former self-centered ways is far more difficult and almost impossible.—*Justifications,* by Guyon.

4

2/26/00

CHAPTER 4:1—*How beautiful you are, my love; how beautiful you are! You have doves' eyes, besides what is hid within. Your hair is as a flock of goats that appear from Mt. Gilead.*

Although you are not yet perfected, the Bridegroom finds you lovelier than ever before. Your faults are no longer blatant sins. They are, rather, defects in your still rather self-contained nature. For although you are lovelier than ever before, you are not convinced of this for your Bridegroom has spurned you from His innermost chamber. The Bridegroom assures you that you are lovely. Your own inward beauty, which is greater than any outer beauty, is still hidden from your eyes.

Your eyes, in faithfulness and simplicity, are like those of doves. Simplicity, so highly recommended in the Scriptures, causes you to act only with God's good pleasure in view. None of your own selfish intentions, motives, or schemes are allowed. When simplicity is perfected within you, you act without

53

giving your actions any unnecessary thought. To act simply with your neighbor is to act sincerely without fanfare or pride. These are the eyes and the heart of the dove that is so dear to Christ.

The hair, representing the affection that springs from the spirit, separates you from earthly ties. Single-hearted love for God rises above the most excellent gifts until it arrives at God Himself. In this way, abandoned love for God resembles the goats that find their way up the steepest mountain.

3/6/00

CHAPTER 4:2—*Your teeth are like a flock of sheep that are evenly shorn and freshly washed; everyone of them bears twins, and none is barren among them.*

The teeth represent the understanding and memory, which serve to chew and digest the things you desire to know. The understanding, memory, and imagination have already been purified. No longer is there any confusion. The teeth are compared to evenly shorn sheep. This praises the simplicity of your oneness with God.

At this point you will be stripped of your own excessive inclination to act out of self-motivation. In spite of this stripping, you are not barren or unfruitful. In fact, you will bear *double* fruit, and better fruit, when your gifts, such as understanding, memory and imagination, become lost in Him rather than being, in themselves, your focal point.

CHAPTER 4:3—*Your lips are like a scarlet thread, and your speech is sweet. Your cheeks are like a piece of pomegranate, besides that which is hidden within.*

The lips represent the will. The will kisses with affection that which it loves. As your will comes to love God alone, all your affection is toward Him. The affections are reunited in a single-hearted love for God. All the strength of the will is given to God.

"Your speech," He adds, "is sweet." The heart has a language that no one but God can understand. Something within you speaks only to Him. There are secrets shared only between the Bridegroom and His bride.

"Your cheeks are like a piece of pomegranate." The pomegranate has many seeds all contained in one single rind. Likewise, all your thoughts are reordered in God by a pure and perfect love. All that has been described here is nothing compared with all that is yet concealed in the deepest depths of your spirit.

CHAPTER 4:4—*Your neck is like the tower of David, built up with bulwarks, a thousand shields hang upon it, all the armor of the mighty men.*

The neck is the strength of the soul. Here the neck is compared to the tower of David because your only true strength is in God. David represents the house of Jesus Christ. Many times in the Psalms,

David reveals that God alone is his support, his refuge, his defense, and his strong tower (Psalm 61).

The bulwarks that surround you are built with the total abandonment that you have toward your Lord. Trust, faith, and hope have strengthened this abandonment. The weaker you are in yourself, the stronger you are in God. A thousand shields hang upon the bulwark to defend against countless enemies. Your enemies are both visible and invisible. The armor of mighty men defends you as you remain in God.

4/3/00

CHAPTER 4:5—*Your two breasts are like two twin gazelles which feed among the lilies.*

You receive help in order to nourish others. Your ability to help others is likened to two twin gazelles: You are ever watchful, and attend quickly to those in need. All help comes from Jesus Christ. Those that come to Him are fed "among the lilies" (that is, with the purity of all that Jesus is).

CHAPTER 4:6—*Until the day break and the shadows flee away, I will get me to the mountains of myrrh and to the hill of frankincense.*

The Bridegroom interrupts His praise of you to invite you to follow Him toward the mountain. This is the mountain where the myrrh grows and the hill where frankincense is collected.

On that day that the Father appears, you shall receive a new life. The shadows which surround you in your naked faith will run away and vanish. Until then you will no longer find Him except in the cross. Yet, this mountain of myrrh will be a sweet taste to God. Your sufferings will rise toward Him as incense. Through your sufferings He will be able to enter into rest within you.

CHAPTER 4:7—*You are all fair, my love, there is no spot in you.*

Until you are immersed in the cross you are still not all fair. Now that you are buried under a load of trouble and affliction, you have become all fair; and there is no spot in you.

You would now be ready for lasting union with God if remnants of your former harsh, unyielding, and limited nature were not still present within you. This is not a fault in you, nor does it offend God. Your old nature, which came from Adam, must be taken away.

As for you, the cross has entirely destroyed your beauty in the eyes of men. In His eyes, however, you are beautiful. You no longer see any beauty in yourself, and this has become your true beauty.

CHAPTER 4:8—*Come from Lebanon, my spouse, come from Lebanon, come; you will be crowned from the top of Amana, from the peak of Shenir and Hermon, from the dens of the lions, from the mountains of the leopards.*

The Bridegroom here calls you by the name of "spouse." He invites you to allow yourself quickly to be united with Him. He calls you to your wedding and your coronation.

But, dear Bridegroom, shall I say it? Why do You so earnestly and continually invite a bride to a consummation that she so passionately desires? You call her from Lebanon though she is in Jerusalem. Do You compare her with the lofty heights of this great mountain? Is she so high in your eyes? She hardly needs to take one step before she is united with You with an everlasting tie. Yet when she approaches your bed she is challenged by sixty strong men. Isn't it cruel to sweetly and powerfully attract her toward a treasure which she values above all else, only to turn her away when she comes closest to her greatest happiness? You invite her, call her, prepare her for marriage, and give her a delicious drink of what she shall obtain, which draws her even more! Then You cause her to suffer greatly by delaying the gift which You have promised!

"Come, my spouse," He says, "for there is but a single step to take before you will be my spouse in reality." Until now He has called you "my fair one, my beloved, my dove," but never "my spouse." How sweet is this name! How much sweeter is the reality of it!

Come from the highest mountain tops (from the

practice of the highest virtues represented by the mountains). However high all that may be to you, you must still come up higher. Come also from the lion's den and from the mountains of the leopards, for you cannot arrive at such a high place without enduring the most cruel persecutions of men and demons. It is time now to rise above everything, since you are prepared to be crowned as His bride. It is at this very summit that you will enter with Him into the bosom of the Father. There you will find true rest, for you will have let go of everything in order to reach that point.

CHAPTER 4:9—*You have wounded my heart, my sister spouse; you have wounded my heart with one glance of your eyes and with one lock of hair that falls upon your neck.*

"You are My sister, since we belong to the same Father. You are My spouse since you are already engaged to me. My sister spouse!" Such sweet words to an anguished bride whose grief overflows because the beautiful One she adores, and who tenderly loves her, cannot be possessed.

He says, "You have wounded my heart!" The Bridegroom looks upon you and sees that all your afflictions and sufferings have not caused you to turn your gaze away from Him. You have taken no notice of your wounds.[1] You are offended by Him in no way. You gaze continually upon your Lord and do not consider your own interests. With undivided love you consider His interests alone. He is the sole object of your affection.

You ask, "How could I have continually beheld Him when I do not even know where He is?" You are not aware that your gaze has become so pure that you have not noticed that you always see Him. You must always forget yourself, and every other created thing,[2] and fix your inward eyes on God alone.[3] Center all your affection in God. Lose your will entirely in His.

CHAPTER 4:10—*How fair are your breasts, my sister spouse! Your breasts are fairer than wine, and the fragrance of your perfume than all spices.*

The Bridegroom foresees all the victories that you will accomplish for Him. He sees how you will spiritually nourish many. The further you advance, the more you are able to nourish others. The Bridegroom continually fills you with the milk of the Word for those in need. This is why He says, "How fair are your breasts, my sister spouse." They are more beautiful than wine for they furnish both wine and milk: one for strong men, and the other for babies.

The fragrance of your perfume, by which many are drawn to the Bridegroom, is better than any spice. There is a fragrance in you that no one will recognize except those that are far advanced; and, in turn, such people will be drawn even more to the Bridegroom through you. This secret perfume will astonish those who do not see this mystery. Nonetheless, they will have to say that it is an irresistible perfume. This fragrance must be the annointing of the Holy Spirit, which the Lord's Christ alone can communicate to His bride.

CHAPTER 4:11—*Your lips, my spouse, drip like a honeycomb: honey and milk are under your tongue; and the fragrance of your garments is like the fragrance of Lebanon.*

You become like a nursing mother. Richness flows from you; your lips drip like a honeycomb to impart sweetness to all you touch. Your own words are not the source of your richness: It is the Bridegroom Himself who is rich within you. Your lips are used by the Bridegroom to speak His Word. He places honey and milk under your tongue so that you may give them to any that lack.

You are all honey to those who are to be won by the sweetness of comfort. You are all milk to those who have become perfectly simple and childlike. The fragrance of your good works clothes you like a garment, filling the air with a sweet smelling perfume.

CHAPTER 4:12—*A garden enclosed is my sister spouse; a garden enclosed, a fountain sealed.*

The Bridegroom praises His bride for no other purpose than to show us what pleases Him. You are shut up like an enclosed garden unto Him. Within and without there is nothing that is not totally for

Him. None of your actions are for anyone besides Him. You are shut up on every side. Intimately united with your Lord, you are also a fountain whose waters replenish the earth. The Bridegroom has kept you sealed so that not a drop will escape without His direction. The water that comes forth from within you is perfectly pure and without pollution for it comes from God.

CHAPTER 4:13—*Your plants are a paradise of pomegranates, with the fruits of the orchard, cypress with spikenard.*

The bride's fruitfulness will be so great that she shall be like a paradise of pomegranates. As the pomegranate gives nourishment to each of its seeds, so the Spirit of God will reveal Himself to His bride in different ways and in different situations.

This passage concerns the work of the church. There are many kinds of fruits in this garden: Each member has common qualities and unique qualities. One excels in love, another in meekness, another in suffering and setting a good example. Still another rests in devotion, recollection, and peace. All are made fruitful by the crucified Bridegroom.

CHAPTER 4:14—*Spikenard and saffron; calamus and cinnamon with all the trees of Lebanon; myrrh and aloes with all the chief ointments.*

The Beloved continues to praise the bride. Many

are drawn to Him through His goodness at work in her. She looks after all those that she brings to Him, and gives to each according to their need.

CHAPTER 4:15—*A fountain of gardens, a well of living water, and streams flowing strongly from Lebanon.*

The Fountain of the gardens is the Lord Himself. Who but Christ is the source of the grace which causes spiritual life to spring up, flourish, and grow? The Bridegroom is a well of living waters. These waters descend from the Bridegroom through the bride. Streams of water flow wildly from the depths of God, represented by Mount Lebanon. These streams overflow the whole earth, which represents all those who truly want to enter into the deep fellowship of Christ. You must be willing to endure the work in order to enjoy the fruits.

CHAPTER 4:16—*Arise, north wind, and come, south wind; blow through my garden and let its spices flow out.*

Invite the Holy Spirit, the Spirit of Life, to come and breathe through you. Desire that your garden be filled with flowers and fruits and that its fragrance draw others to Him. The Bridegroom wants your resurrection to be quick so that you might receive new life by the breath of the Spirit. The Spirit will bring you to life.

Notes To Chapter Four

1. I have already stated that these wounds are, within, the apparent desertion of the Bridegroom (which is the most agonizing of the soul's sufferings) and without, they are the persecuting malice of men and devils.—*Justifications*.

2. During the whole time of the Bridegroom's apparent absence, the spouse is neither occupied with self nor with the world; she is farther than ever from such unfaithfulness; she thinks she has lost the presence of her Well-beloved—and is not her continual grief for this seeming loss a perpetual presence?—*Justifications*.

3. This fixedness of the interior eye upon Christ must be unfailingly preserved, though unconsciously; thus the spouse never forgets her Bridegroom. Remark too, that the inattention of the spouse to self has its sole origin and cause in her unremitting application of her heart to her Lord, and she is thus free from the mistake of those who put Him out of mind that they may sin without restraint.—*Justifications*.

5

CHAPTER 5:1—*Let my beloved come into his garden and eat the fruit of his apple trees. I am come into my garden, my sister spouse, I have gathered my myrrh with spice; I have eaten my honeycomb with my honey. I have drunk my wine with my milk. Eat, friends, drink and be drunken, dearly beloved.*

You are like a beautiful garden full of flowers and fruits. Beg your Beloved to come and enjoy His garden. You cannot enjoy your garden apart from Him. "Come into your garden and take everything for yourself and for those with whom You want to share its fruit."

The Bridegroom happily enters into the garden of His beloved. He partakes of everything, but He wants you to see that He Himself eats first from the table that He has spread for His friends.

He has gathered the myrrh for you; the myrrh is the suffering that you will encounter in your Christian walk. Still, the myrrh is bundled with pleasant spices. The spices are for the Bridegroom; the myrrh is for the bride.

The Bridegroom eats the sweets of love. Charmed with His bride's generosity, He invites all His friends to eat and drink beside His bride. You are a garden full of fruit, and watered with milk and honey. Through Him you have an abundant supply for the spiritual needs of all.

The church invites Christ to come and eat of her fruit. The Bridegroom did, indeed, come into His garden when He became flesh. He gathered His myrrh with His spices even before His bride did. He suffered the bitterness of His passion which sent up a sweet perfume to His Father.

Jesus has eaten His honeycomb with His honey. He practices what He preaches, and does not ask of you anything that He has not first endured. Through His grace you are able to do all that He asks of you. The life of Christ is like a honeycomb within you. The sweetness of the honeycomb is the food, indeed the happiness, He shares with His Father.

"I have drunk my wine with my milk," says the Beloved. "What wine were You able to drink, dear Lord, that caused you to entirely forget Yourself?" "The wine of My overpowering love for you." The Lord forgot about Himself and thought only of His people's salvation. Full of love, He bore reproaches and mockery; He gave His own flesh and blood. The wine of the last supper is the nourishment of His passion. The wine is His divinity; the milk is His humanity. In Christ the two are mixed together.

The Savior invites all that belong to Him to share His sufferings and reproaches with Him. His example is like wine and milk. Wine gives strength and courage to perform God's will. Milk is the sweet teachings of Jesus.

You are invited to hear and imitate Jesus Christ.

CHAPTER 5:2—*I sleep, but my heart is awake. It is the voice of my beloved that knocks, saying, "Open to me, my sister, my love, my dove, my undefiled; for my head is filled with dew, and my locks with the drops of the night."*

Although your outer man may seem dead like a body in a deep sleep, your spirit keeps a secret and hidden union with God. As you mature as a Christian you may experience God operating in you more powerfully in the night than during the day.

While asleep you clearly hear the voice of your Beloved calling within you. He longs to make Himself heard. "I come to you, my love, whom I have chosen above all others to be my bride. You are my dove in simplicity—my perfect one, my beautiful, my undefiled. See that my head is filled with all that I have suffered for you. I have been drenched with the drops of the cruelest persecutions. I come now to you. Will you join Me in bearing suffering and reproach and even confusion?"[1]

Until now you have only tasted the bitterness of the cross; now you will experience its confusion and

67

disgrace. Each experience is different from the other: All are terrible.

CHAPTER 5:3—*I have taken off my coat; how can I put it back on? I have washed my feet; how can I dirty them?*[2]

You see that your Bridegroom wishes to make you a partaker of His sufferings, and you are sadly afraid. You are disheartened at the disgrace you must bear. Although before, you boldly and courageously accepted the cross, you are not so willing to bear its infamy and disgrace.

You are afraid of two things in viewing this coming disgrace. One, will you be overcome by the things you have thrown aside—that is, yourself and your natural weakness? Second, will you be caught up in caring for the creation more than the Creator?[3]

You, like the maiden, have put off your old ways, your faults, and your old life. How can you put them on again? Nothing else can cause you such deep humiliation and confusion. When people hate you with cause, it is easy to bear; for you trust that the persecution will glorify God. You are already pure in your affections, completely devoted to your Beloved. How can you go back into the paths of the world?

Poor blind one! What are you fighting against? The Bridegroom only wants to test your faithfulness and see if you are really ready to do His will. He was despised and rejected of men, smitten of God and afflicted (Isaiah 53). He who was innocence itself was numbered with the sinners. But you, though loaded down with guilt, cannot bear to be accused of evil!

You will find it difficult to resist His call to share in His sufferings, no matter how much you loathe the disgrace that may come with opposition and persecution.

CHAPTER 5:4—*My beloved put his hand through the opening, and my heart leaped at his touch.*

The Beloved, despite your resistance, puts His hand in the little opening of self-abandonment which is still within you.[4] As you come to this point you will refuse nothing that God asks. But when He reveals His plan in every detail and claims the right to your obedience, though you are lovingly overwhelmed by His touch deep within, yet you find trouble where you expect none. You tremble at His touch and feel the anguish of what His will requires of you.[5] Job said, "Have pity on me, my friends, for the hand of God has touched me" (Job 19:21). So, likewise, you tremble under the touch of God.

How jealous you are, dear Lord, for your bride to do your will! How can a simple excuse offend you so deeply! Couldn't you have stopped your dear and faithful one from resisting You?[6]

All this is necessary for your perfection. Your

Bridegroom allows you to see your fault in order that He might free you from your complacency. You have reached a certain degree of purity and innocence. Do not rest in that. To some degree you have been stripped of your own righteousness. The only righteousness you have is in your Bridegroom; yet you are still attached to this measure of righteousness, and you are tempted to take credit for His life within you.

CHAPTER 5:5—*I rose to open to my beloved; my hands dripped with myrrh, and my fingers were bathed with the choicest myrrh.*

As soon as you recognize your fault you quickly run to repent. Renew your commitment to abandonment! Yet this sacrifice will not happen without pain and bitterness. Your weak nature will be racked with pain, and the distress you feel will be beyond anything that you have yet experienced.

CHAPTER 5:6—*I withdrew the bolt of my door for my beloved; but he had turned aside and disappeared. My soul melted when he spoke; I looked for him, but did not find him; I called him, but He gave no answer.*

Now all barriers that have stood between you and your Beloved are removed. For how can you be fully united to your Lord without your total submission? To remove the final barrier is the most courageous abandonment and the purest sacrifice in all heaven and earth.

You open to your Beloved,[7] thinking that He will come in and heal the grief caused by His touch. But the blow would be too mild if the cure were so quickly applied! He hides, He flies away, He turns aside and disappears. The Bridegroom leaves you with nothing but the pain caused by your impurity and procrastination.

The Bridegroom is so good, however, that even when He hides Himself He continues to give you great favor. The longer and more severe the trials are, the more He does this.

Even now He is doing this within you and you do not even know it! You melt when He speaks, and through this softening you lose your hard and stubborn characteristics.[8] And when the Bridegroom cannot be found, you will know unbelievable pain.

CHAPTER 5:7—*The watchmen that went about the city found me. They hit me and wounded me; the keepers of the wall took away my veil from me.*

What inconceivable suffering! Nothing like this has ever happened to you before. Before, the Bridegroom had openly protected you, and you lived under His protection. Now He has gone away and it is your fault! What has happened? You thought you had already suffered much through the many trials that had tested your faithfulness to God. These were small matters compared to the suffering you must

71

now experience. All that you have suffered so far is but the shadow of suffering. You had no reason to expect any less.

Do you think you can be united to a God covered with wounds, torn with nails, and stripped of everything, without being treated the same way? You will find yourself "wounded by those who keep the walls of the city." These keepers are anyone whom God uses whether they be men or demons. Before, your enemies had not dared to attack even though they watched you continually. Now the "keepers" wound you and take away the covering of your own self-righteousness.

What will you do in your unutterable sadness? The Bridegroom will have nothing more to do with you after you have been so severely wounded by soldiers. You have lost your veiling to the keepers. You will be called mad if you continue to seek your Beloved in such a condition. Yet if you do not look for Him you will die of longing. Has anyone known such agony?

CHAPTER 5:8—*I charge you, daughters of Jerusalem, if you find my Beloved, tell Him that I am lovesick.*

True love has no eyes for itself.[9] Forget your bleeding wounds and your loss, and think only of Him. Seek Him with your whole heart, no matter what obstacle stands in your way. In your weakness you may call out to other inward believers. He will certainly show Himself to the others whom He loves.

Your words are few: "Tell Him that I am love-sick." Shouldn't you, fair woman, tell Him of your wounds and all that you have endured to find Him? No! All you can do is tell Him that you are sick with love. You are so wounded within that you are insensible to all other external pains. They are even a delight by comparison.

CHAPTER 5:9—*Why is your beloved better than any other love, most beautiful among women? Why is your beloved better than any other love, that you ask this of us?*

The daughters of Jerusalem do not cease to call you the most beautiful among women. Your painful wounds are hidden, and the ones that are exposed add to your beauty. They are amazed to find so strong a love—a constant and faithful love—in the middle of so many disasters. The daughters ask, "Who is your Beloved?" They know He must be incomparably handsome to capture you; yet they do not yet understand how straight and how naked is the path of faith.

You, however, see no beauty in yourself. "Do not call me fair" (Ruth 1:20). Perhaps you could call attention to yourself, but your search for Him is your all-consuming concern. You think nothing of yourself: If you knew you would plunge over a cliff in your search, you would not be stopped. Your resistance to total abandonment through fear of becoming covered with the dirt of the world has cost you dearly: Your Bridegroom is gone. Your beauty and welfare no longer matter: You look only for Him.

CHAPTER 5:11—*His head is as the most fine gold, his locks as the cluster of the palm, black as a raven.*

The locks of hair covering His head are to be understood as the humanity which covers the divinity of Christ. His humanity, revealed on the cross, is like the cluster of the palm. As He died there for mankind, He won a victory over your enemies and obtained for you the fruits of His redemption. These fruits came through His death. Then the bud of the palm tree opened, and the church emerged from the heart of the Bridegroom. There His humanity appeared as black as a raven—covered with wounds and loaded with the sins and blackness of all men. All this blackness was placed upon His unrivaled whiteness and purity.

Christ appeared as a reproach of men. He was despised by all men (Psalm 23:6). Was He not black? And yet the blackness set off His beauty. Blackness was put on Him so that it might be taken off the whole world.

CHAPTER 5:12—*His eyes are like a dove's by the rivers of waters, washed with milk, and sitting beside overflowing streams.*

The bride holds up the perfect qualities of her Bridegroom for all to see. His rich nature and His wonderful qualities are your joy in the midst of your misery.

Your Lord's eyes are pure, innocent, and simple; His knowledge is free from every corruption. Your Beloved's eyes are not those of a common dove's. His eyes are washed in the milk of divine grace. The grace of God rests on Him without measure, filling Him with the wisdom and knowledge of God (Colossians 2:3). He rests beside the small streams that pass through the lowly of heart. Even if you are not far advanced, you will not be disagreeable to Him. He lives in all our hearts, but He desires most to live in abandoned hearts, near those rapid and overflowing streams that are hindered by nothing that is set before them. These streams rush forward with even greater intensity when an obstacle tries to stop them.

CHAPTER 5:13—*His cheeks are as a bed of spices, prepared by the perfumers; his lips are like lilies, dropping choice myrrh.*

As the cheeks are part of the head, so the humanity of Christ is united with His divinity. The cheeks represent the soul of Jesus, and the beds of spices are His perfectly human mind, will, and emotion. Truly a skilled artisan, the Holy Spirit of God chose and arranged them in the Man Christ Jesus.

The lips are compared to the red lilies of Syria— exceedingly beautiful flowers. What lips could be fairer or sweeter than those that give words of spirit and life? They also bring forth an attitude of repentence and willingness to die to yourself.

CHAPTER 5:14—*His legs are as pillars of marble set in sockets of fine gold; his face is as Lebanon, excellent as the cedars.*

The whole lower part of the body, the legs and feet, represent the flesh of Christ. The marble symbolizes His incorruptibility. For a few hours He yielded to death, but because He was united with His Father (set in sockets of gold), He did not see corruption. The wonderful House of God, sustained by His incorruptible Word, will never be dissolved.

His face is as beautiful as Lebanon. The saints are planted in Him like a forest of cedars. He is the One elected for all, and He elects all men. No one is elected unless He chooses them, and He has predestined all that shall be conformed to His image. He is the first-born among many brothers (Romans 8:29).

CHAPTER 5:16—*His throat is most sweet, yes, he is altogether lovely. This is my beloved, and this is my friend, daughters of Jerusalem.*

Good qualities can be complimented, but some qualities are so admirable that they are above all praise. Such is the Bridegroom. His perfections are without number; He makes His bride speechless when she tries to tell of His worth.

Her passion causes her to burst out into praise of His excellence. Having tried to express the inexpressible, she suddenly becomes silent. She ends her impassioned speech which her love has prompted. She invites her friends to love the One who is most dear to her. But now her silence is preceded by these few words: "His throat is sweet."

The throat is the organ of speech. Jesus is the expression of God. He is altogether lovely! Who can explain His loveliness? The bride tells her companions, "Do not believe me because I have told you of my Beloved—taste and see for yourself." He possesses rare beauty—beauty beyond compare—beauty that cannot be expressed. So see why I am sick with love.

CHAPTER 5:17—*Where has your beloved gone, fairest among women? Where has your beloved turned aside, so that we might seek him with you?*

In your abandonment you become a great missionary. You preach His perfection, His sweetness, and His unending loveliness. You inspire others to seek Him and find Him for themselves. All conquering Love! How wonderful are your victories! You, impetuous as a torrent in your love, carry along everyone that You meet. Who would not want to seek so desirable a love?

Notes To Chapter Five

1. Thus it appears that the spiritual one's whole course is but a constant succession of crosses, ignominy, and confusion. There are many persons who abandon themselves to certain crosses, but not to all; who can never prevail upon themselves to be willing that their reputation in the sight of men should be taken away. This is the very point God is here aiming at.

   The bride feels, too, an extreme repugnance to obeying the command of God to apply herself without; she has become fond of her inward retreat. Nevertheless, it is quite certain that she will not bear these crosses unless she leaves her solitude. When God intends that some followers of His shall really die to self, He sometimes permits in them certain apparent, but not real, false steps, by the effect of which their reputation among men is destroyed.

   I once knew an interior person to whom a host of most terrible crosses was foreshown, and among them the loss of reputation, to which she was exceedingly attached. She could not bring herself to give this up, and begged of God any other cross but that, thus formally refusing her consent. She herself told me that she had ever since remained in the same position. So fatal was this reservation to her progress, that she had been favored by our Lord with neither humiliations nor graces since that time.—*Justifications.*

2. The soul cannot remain long in this state of nakedness and spoliation, and hence the Apostle (Col.3:9,10) informs us that after being stripped of the old Adam, we must put on the new man Christ Jesus. Having renounced and abandoned everything, even our attachment to things good in themselves, and having learned to will neither this nor that, nor anything but what the Lord's will proposes to us, we must now be clothed again with the same love of God and fellowship with Him; but no longer because this is pleasant, expedient, or fitted to gratify our self-love, but because it is pleasing to God, expedient for His honor, and fitted to

advance His glory.—*The Love of God,* by St. Francis of Sales.

3. In order to strengthen the spirit of the believer, God makes use of what John of the Cross styles *the obscure night of the spirit,* in which He permits the defects which the believer supposed vanished and forever gone to reappear in strongly marked features on the surface. I refer to natural faults of temper, hasty words or acts, caprices of conduct, rebellious thoughts. God then strips him of his facility in practicing divine virtues and good works, all his imperfections reappear, and he suffers on every side. God lays His hand heavily upon him; others slander him and subject him to persecutions; his own thoughts are thoughts of rebellion, and the devils besiege him besides. It is by this terrible array of crucifying instruments that the Christian is made to succumb and yield to death. If any one of them were missing, the part not thus assaulted would serve as a refuge and reprieve; and, for all his good intentions, the Christian would continue in his life of self.

These defects are not voluntary, nor are the thousand wretched weaknesses that assault the believer and make him miserable; but of this the Christian is not always conscious, as the absence of God leads him to think that his faults are the cause.

Does the bride turn towards Him? She finds herself cast off and experiences nothing but His indignation. Does she look at self within? Temptations, wretchedness, poverty, imperfection? Does she look imploringly towards the world? These are thorns that pierce and repel her. She is suspended, as it were, at a distance from God *and* the world; and to complete her misery, she finds that He commonly thrusts these poor suffering ones at such times out of doors, i.e. He makes it necessary in the order of his providence that they should leave their solitude and mix in the commerce of the world. Their greatest torment is that, while they ardently desire to be wholly detached from the world, they find their hearts continually going out after it, in spite of their utmost exertions. But now at last, when the world and their own defects, the strength of God's arm, their experience of their own weakness, and the malice of men and devils have worked out the purposes of God, He delivers them, at a single stroke, from every foe and receives them, perfectly pure, into Himself. Those who will not consent to this crucifying process must be content to remain all their lifetime in self and imperfection.

The spouse means here to explain that in the beginning the young Christian suffers persecutions and calumny with resolution, from an inward and powerful sustaining consciousness that they are undeserved. But here this is no longer the case. As the Christian grows in the Lord, he becomes sensitive to every thought of sin. In consequence, he feels that he is the most miserable creature in the world, is persuaded that he deserves all his agonies, and is covered with the most inexpressible confusion and humiliation. He is convinced that there is no one so wicked as he. And the greater his former detachment from the world and from selfish enjoyment of spiritual blessing, the more he now feels his wretchedness, his ties to earth and its heavy weight, and all in so distressing a degree that he is thrown into an agony a thousand times a day. He seems to have an appetite for every pleasure and to long to enjoy them all, though, in fact, he shuns them more than ever.

I remarked previously that at this time the Christian was thrust out into active life; that is, that his situation or unforseen circumstances obliged him to mingle with the world. He had hitherto withdrawn into solitude, painfully separating himself from the world; and it is now very distressing to return to it again. Still, if God did not require him to live a normal life in the world, he would never know who he really was; nor could he ever be made sufficiently acquainted with his own weakness and his absolute dependance upon grace, nor recognize that he can expect nothing from himself, but must wait upon God for everything, must trust in Him, despair of self, hate self, and quit it forever. This pain and suffering is not experienced by those who know not God, nor by those who give themselves up to license. They cannot feel the sting of the evil to which they voluntarily subject themselves, quenching the Holy Spirit, and forgetting God. The longer they live, the more depraved they become, while believers, after having been tempted, proved and tried, are deemed worthy, on account of their *unconscious faithfulness*, of being received into God.—*Justifications.*

4. It is important to bear in mind here what was said in the beginning, that there is a voluntary resistance which puts an absolute stop to the work of God, because he cannot violate man's freedom of will, and that there is also a resistance of nature, which lies indeed in the will, but without being voluntary, it is the repugnance of nature to its own destruction. But whatever may be the extent of this repugnance, and how great may be the rebellion of nature against its own annihilation, God does not cease his effectual working to that end, taking advantage of the consecration the Christian has made and the total abandonment which he has never withdrawn, and does not now withdraw, his will remaining submissive and subdued to God, notwithstanding the rebellion in his feelings. It is this abandonment, this submission of the will, which is concealed in the very depths of the believer and is sometimes unrecognized by him, which I have called the passage of the hand of God; for it is by this means that He is able to continue His purifying operations in us, without violating our freedom.—*Justifications.*

5. When I speak of God's unfolding his plans in detail, we must not understand that He points out to the Christian such and such things to be renounced and sacrificed; not at all. I have often said that, with God, speaking is doing, and so here, He only explains his designs by putting his follower into the crucible of the most severe trials, as will be seen. He brings him to the point of sacrificing to Him not only his possessions but his entire being, and not only for time but for eternity. And how is this sacrifice accomplished? By an absolute despair of self, which takes away every support in human strength and forces unconditional aban-

donment of the believer into the hands of God. For we must remember that the more we despair of self, the more we trust in God, though always in a way recognized by the intellect. The further removed we are from certainty and a faith resting on sight, the more deeply we enter into the faith of God, stripped of every support. The more we hate self the better we love God. Whenever God takes anything away from a Christian, it is a sacrifice, but the last sacrifice of all, the one which I am in the habit of describing as the *pure sacrifice,* is that made by the believer when, finding himself abandoned of God, of self and of the world, cries out to Him, *My God, why hast Thou forsaken me?* (Matt. 27:46), and immediately adds with the Lord Jesus, *Into thy hands I commend my spirit* (Luke 23:46). This was the entire and absolute sacrifice of Himself, and it is this surrender of the whole of self for time and eternity which I call the last sacrifice; after this, those further words of the Lord Jesus, *It is finished* (John 19:30), announce the completion of the soul's sacrifice, and close the scene.

All our troubles spring from our resistance, which springs from our attachments. The more we torment ourselves when in suffering, the sharper it becomes; but if we surrender ourselves to it more and more and permit the crucifying process to go on undisturbed, it is much softened. We see and recognize the hindrances to our spiritual progress only as they are removed.—*Justifications.*

6. The resistance here spoken of is of two kinds, which have respect to the demands made by God in the preceding verses. We have heard the voice of the Bridegroom, saying to his spouse, *Open to me, my sister spouse!* for I am heavy with the drops of my passion. The bride then sees clearly that He has come to her, loaded with grief, to make her a partaker of his suffering; for his addresses are painful impressions, produced by Himself in her, of all possible grief, attended by all conceivable weakness; for if she could be strong in her suffering, she would bear it gladly. God opens to her the possibility of loss of reputation and of slanderous persecutions, and follows it up with the reality; He

accompanies these troubles with a sense of her own innumerable frailties and wretchedness, an apparent loss of virtue, or rather of strength and facility for good works, so that she is covered with inconceivable confusion and distress. Finally, without specification or reserve, and without any distinct view, she will surrender to the rigors of the Divine Justice, and God takes her at her word.

While the trial lasts, the heart feels an extreme rebellion against the suffering; it can find no trace of abandonment within; it cries with all its strength for deliverance. In the moments of calm which sometimes appear, its appreciation and love of the Divine Justice returns, and it cannot refrain from renewing its sacrifice at the altar of the same Justice, until the tempest recommences.—Then it forgets again its sacrifice and its love of Justice, and devoured by its repugnances seems to experience the pangs of death.

At other times, before subjecting the believer to trials, God sets before him without detail the most extreme sufferings, and requires his consent. Some refuse, not being able to yield the sacrifice; some absolutely, others for a few days only. And their resistance causes them horrible torments, especially if they had previously been yielding and obedient, and were unconsciously sullied by a secret pride in their faithfulness in suffering, and in never having refused anything to God, however exacting His requirements.

God permits the bride to resist the sacrifice upon the Cross and to feel repugnance to receiving a Bridegroom covered with blood and steeped in grief. But devotees of this stamp seldom resist long. The resistance is necessary to convince them of their frailty and to prove to them how far they are from possessing the courage they fondly imagined. There are some of them, who, after having had an exquisitely pure experience of the delights of love, find themselves exceedingly feeble when Love presents its crucifying demands; and if they have previously been faithful, the pain of the spiritual impurity contracted by this resistance causes them great suffering.—*Justifications.*

7. This *opening* is a renewed abandonment; the resistance lately exhibited having interrupted its course, the soul must make a new and express act of abandonment. God always exacts this, and it marks that the soul has been unfaithful, since it has need to turn again and renew its overt and perceptible acts.—*Justifications.*

8. *My heart,* says David, speaking in the person of our Lord Jesus Christ upon the cross, *my heart is like wax; it is melted in the midst of my bowels.* The heart of the Savior, that oriental pearl, precious above all others, and of inestimable value, cast into an unspeakably corrosive sea of bitterness in the day of his passion, melted within Him, was dissolved and ran away in anguish under the pressure of such intolerable agonies.

   But love is stronger than death, and can touch the heart and soften and melt it more quickly than any other power. *My soul melted when He spake,* says the spouse; and what does she mean to express by this but that her soul was no longer contained within herself, but had flowed towards her Divine Lover. God commanded Moses to speak to the rock and it should bring forth water (*Numb.* 20:8); what wonder, then, if when He himself speaks softly, the soul of His spouse should melt within her. Balsam is naturally so thick that it will neither pour nor flow, and the more closely and the longer it is kept the thicker it becomes, until it is found at last red, hard and transparent; but by heat it is dissolved and rendered fluid. Love had liquified the Bridegroom, and hence the spouse calls Him *an oil poured forth;* and now her turn has come, and she proclaims herself as melted with love. My soul, says she, ran down while my Beloved spake. The love of the Bridegroom was in her heart and under her breasts like new wine, exceeding strong, which cannot be restrained within its vat, but runs over on every side.—*The Love of God,* by St. Francis of Sales

9. I have seen three pious men injuriously treated. The first buried his sufferings in silence, through fear of the Divine Righteousness. The second rejoiced on his own account,

hoping for the recompense of reward, but was afflicted for him that had done him wrong. The third, entirely forgetful of self, wept at the injury which his oppressor had inflicted upon himself by wrong doing. Behold here three worthy champions in the lists of virtue! One impelled by fear, another stimulated by the hope of reward, and a third inspired by the disinterested breathings of perfect love.— *Sacred Ladder,* by St. John Climachus.

6

CHAPTER 6:1—*My beloved is gone down into his garden, to the beds of spices, to feed in the gardens and to gather lilies.*

After your long search you have at last heard the news of your Beloved! Once you confidently declared that you would hold Him so firmly that He would never escape, but He has gone farther away than ever before!

You did not see how presumptuous you were to think you could control Him. He gives Himself or withdraws Himself, as seems good to Him. His bride should will only as He wills, and allow Him to come and go as He pleases. Do you see how you preferred your own pleasure in loving and possessing Him? If you ever see Him again, you will let Him come and go as He pleases.

Still, you know that He is "gone down into His garden." Deep within you there is a place reserved totally for Him. A sweet fragrance fills this place where God lives within you. There He comes to feed on what belongs to Him alone. Nothing there belongs to you. He finds pleasure in the garden which He has planted, cultivated and caused to bear fruit. So let Him gather His lilies! Let all your purity be for Him! Let Him have all the pleasures and profit from your garden!

CHAPTER 6:2—*I am my beloved's, and my beloved is mine: he feeds among the lilies.*

The moment you are freed from all self-seeking you will know a more complete union with God than ever before. Now you belong completely to your Beloved. You have given yourself to Him without reserve. At last you have learned many things about your Beloved. No longer are you bold enough to say you will never let Him go. But now you know Him more deeply than ever. You will never lose Him! Who would not celebrate this with you?

You are so fully your Beloved's that nothing stops you from being lost in Him. Now you are so melted by the warmth of His love that you are ready to be poured into Him.[1]

You are totally His, and He is yours. You experience His goodness with unspeakable delight. He repays your pain with the gentlest affection; He feeds upon your purity.

CHAPTER 6:3—*You are beautiful, my love, sweet and lovely as Jerusalem, terrible as an army prepared for war.*

The Bridegroom sees that you are free from your self-seeking nature. He admires your beauty: "You are as beautiful as Jerusalem." You have lost everything of your own to devote yourself to Him. He has adorned you with all that is His and made you a co-owner of His inheritance. You are a worthy dwelling place for Him, and you desire Him to dwell in you.

As beautiful as you are to Christ, you are frightening to the devil. Sin is threatened by your presence. Your enemies flee from you, though you do not even strike one blow. The enemies of God fear you because you are united with Him.

Pity those who fight their entire lives and achieve no victory! Give yourself to God! Abandon yourself to Him, and you will be more formidable an opponent than an army ready for war.

CHAPTER 6:4—*Turn your eyes away from me because they have made me run away. Your hair is as a flock of goats that appear from Gilead.*

It is difficult to comprehend how deeply God loves you and how pure He wants to make you as His bride. Just when you think you have been perfected, you discover how imperfect you are. Up until now the Bridegroom was glad that His bride never turned her eyes away from Him. Now He does not want you to look at Him. He tells you that your eyes have made Him run away.

You must even lose your perceptible sense of the sight of God. It is possible to look at something until it comes so close that you can no longer focus on it. Your spiritual journey is like this. As you approach deeper and deeper union with God, your union with Him will be hidden from your sight. You can no longer observe yourself, but only what God wants you to see. All is seen by His eyes: especially your inmost heart. Know that it is impossible to love Him too much.

As you become more closely united with God you experience increasing oneness with Him. Marriage between a man and a woman is a faint image of this. Two become one but maintain their essential identity. Complete union between you and your Lord is slow and gradual. Your experience with Him deepens after you have endured much molding and shaping. You never become God—you only know Him in ever-increasing depth.

CHAPTER 6:5—*Your teeth are as a flock of freshly washed sheep. Every one of them bears twins, and there is not one who is barren among them.*

The Bridegroom tells you again what He has already mentioned. But now you walk in the full reality of that which had only been a seed. Your teeth—that is, all the aspects of your soul—are innocent, pure, and clean.

Each part of you is perfectly attuned to the will of your Bridegroom. All that you do bears fruit without being disorderly or ill-timed. Everything you do is doubly blessed.

CHAPTER 6:6—*Your cheeks are like the red rind of a pomegranate; still more is hidden within.*

The rind of the pomegranate, though brightly colored, is nothing compared to the fruit within. So it is with you: Outward appearances count little. It is what is concealed within that counts. Inwardly you are filled with love and grace. This is hidden under a very common exterior. For God likes to hide away the ones He chooses for Himself. Men are not worthy to know them. Angels respect them no matter how humble they appear in the eyes of the world. Those who judge by outward appearance see them as ordinary people. To God, they are a delight.

These hidden ones do not astonish the world with their miracles or extraordinary gifts. God hides them for Himself. He is so jealous of them that He will not expose them to the eyes of men.[2] Instead, He seals them with His seal—they are a fountain sealed with Himself (Ch. 4:12).

But why does He seal them? Because love is as strong as death, and jealousy is as cruel as the grave (Ch. 8:6). How completely the matter is expressed:

Love, like death, ultimately snatches everything away from the soul and conceals it in the hidden places of your spirit. God's jealousy is as cruel as hell—it will spare no means to fully possess you.

You must not be so hidden that you do not help those around you. In doing so, however, you will endure much humiliation. Sometimes people will see you are able to help them, but this will not be the norm. God will hide you away from the admiration of others. He will even let others be offended by you so that after God has finished His plan to use you for their benefit, they will then turn away from you.

The Bridegroom, in this way, treats His bride like Himself. Were not all those He won to His Father offended by Him at one point or another? (Mark 14:27). Look at the life of Christ—externally was there anyone more ordinary than He? Those who do more extraordinary things are like the saints that Jesus said would do greater works than He (John 14:12). Christ is a stumbling block to the Jews and foolishness to the Greeks (I Corinthians 1:23). Simple believers offend those who are legalistic. The gospel is simple, but it is inwardly known. There is more within the gospel than one sees at first glance. The pomegranate has a rind that is nothing to look at, but within is luscious fruit.

CHAPTER 6:7—*There are sixty queens and eighty concubines, and virgins without number.*

There are many that belong to the Bridegroom, and each knows Him to a different degree. Some have made some progress toward Him, and others have just begun to sigh after Him. And there are those who have completely given themselves to God. These are the ones who find their greatest joy in the Bridegroom. He also finds His greatest delight in them.

CHAPTER 6:8—*My dove, my undefiled, is but one; she is the only child of her mother. She is the choice one of her mother. The daughters saw her and blessed her; the queens and the concubines praised her.*

In every generation God looks for people who are like the dove—people who are dove-like in their simplicity and total trust in Him. You have been made one within through the restoration of your soul. You walk in oneness with the Spirit of God. You are free from yourself, and released from the cramped and limited quarters you have lived in. Within, you are perfect. You have lost all of your self-seeking nature.

Until now the Bridegroom has never called you one and perfect; for these qualities are found only in God, and are only fully shared with you after you have been prepared for it.

You are the only child of your mother because you are one with the purpose of God, and you have turned aside from every other way. You, as a member of His bride, are favored of God. You come out of Him in order that you might lose yourself in His bosom.

Inward believers know you, even if you are hidden by God. These inward believers are blessed and delighted each time they see you. Even those who are not so advanced praise you highly for they feel the grace which flows through you.

But the crowds are fickle. Those who bless you one day may count you a criminal the next. So it was with Jesus, so will it be with all who follow Him.

CHAPTER 6:9—*Who is she that comes forth as the sun rising, fair as the moon, clear as the sun, and terrible as an army in battle array?*

A chorus praises the bride of Jesus. Who is this one who comes forth, rising gradually like the sun? Your progress toward God comes a little at a time. His life is perfected in you degree by degree. You rise in God without notice, like the dawn breaking. You are as fair as the moon, for all your light is a reflection of the sun. You are as clear as the sun for you are in union with God. Christ has made you a partaker of His glory and has plunged you into God. Yet to demons, sin, and the world you are terrible and fearful like an army prepared for battle.

CHAPTER 6:10—*I went down into the garden of nuts to see the fruits of the valley; I went to see whether the vine flourished and the pomegranate budded.*

You are not so advanced that you do not cast some backward glances at yourself. But such looks are rare and come only from your humanity. The Bridegroom may permit this slight fault to warn you how harmful self-reflection can be. You want to see if you are producing fruit. Is your vine flowering? This is a reasonable request, isn't it?

CHAPTER 6:11—*I knew nothing; my soul troubled me on account of the chariots of Aminadab.*

When you look for fruit you do not intend to displease your Beloved. But as soon as you look around at yourself you run into trouble. The chariots of Aminadab—thousands of self-reflections—spin through your head and overwhelm you. Only your Beloved sustains you through this attack.

CHAPTER 6:12—*Return, return, Shulamite! Return, return that we may look at you.*

Your return to your Beloved is as sincere and quick as your fault had been slight and unintentional. The mistake had been so slight that your friends did not notice that you had wandered away. You had been declaring your Bridegroom's beauty and suddenly you disappeared from sight. Enamored by your beauty, your companions beg you to return to tell them more of your Beloved.

Notes To Chapter Six

1. As the Bridegroom had spread abroad His love and His soul in the heart of the bride, so she in turn pours her soul into the heart of her Beloved.—As a snowbank upon a hillside exposed to the sun comes forth from itself, quits its form and melts and runs away on the side on which the warmth-giving rays fall upon it, so the soul of the spouse melted and ran toward the voice of her Well-beloved, coming forth from self and the confinement of nature to follow Him who has called her.

   But how is this holy melting of the spouse into her Beloved accomplished? Her extreme delight in her Bridegroom produces in her a spiritual melting of the power to dwell in self; and thus, like melted balsam, deprived of consistency and solidity, her very being runs and flows into Him whom she loves. She does not dart by a sudden effort, nor does she cling and clasp as though she would by force become united, but she only flows gently along like a limpid and liquid thing, into the Divinity she adores. And as we see the clouds, thickened and driven by the south wind, melt and turn into rain, and no longer able to contain themselves, fall and run upon the ground, mingling with and tempering the earth so that they become but one with it; so the bride, who, though loving, was yet dwelling in self, issues forth in this holy and blessed stream, quitting self forever, not only to be united to her Beloved but to be wholly mingled and made one with Him.—*The Love of God,* by St. Francis of Sales.

2. One reason for the jealousy of God is the small number of persons who consecrate themselves to Him without reserve. He cannot bear a rival; hence He takes but little delight in divided hearts. But those who are entirely devoted to Him, He loves and regards as His own peculiar property. With these, He exercises all His rights over them without being interfered with by their freedom of will, since their abandonment is frank, hearty and perfectly voluntary. But He is also seized with a jealousy proportioned to his love. He

cannot abide a spot in them; they are his choice specimens locked up in his own secret drawers, and not exposed to the curious gaze of an unappreciating world.—*Justifications.*

7

CHAPTER 7:1—*What will you see in the Shulamite, but the companies of camps? How beautiful are your feet with shoes, prince's daughter! The joints of your thighs are like jewels, the work of the hands of a master workman.*

There are many who would try to interrupt the precious time between Jesus and His bride. Christ requests that His beloved be not disturbed. He asks these disturbers why they want to look at His bride so much! "What will you see," He asks. His bride has grace and beauty. He has kissed her and increased her purity. At the same time she has the strength and terror of an army. She has become like her Beloved, and the enemies of God fear her.

Your steps are blessed both within and without. All within is beautiful because you continually advance toward God. Each advancement toward God is true rest. Nothing stops your progress. Actually, the greater the rest, the more you progress; and the greater the progress, the more tranquil is your rest.

Your outer steps are also full of beauty. Your path is well ordered for it is found in God's will and directed by His wisdom. Each step you take is in the will of God. He shapes you in the furnace of His love.

CHAPTER 7:2—*Your navel is like a round goblet which never lacks wine. Your waist is like a heap of wheat set about with lilies.*

The navel represents the part of you which is made to grow and be filled up in God. This capacity is not only for you but so that others may be born and brought forth in Jesus Christ. You are able both to receive from the Bridegroom and to administer His grace to those in need. You are continually full of the grace that flows from the fountain of God. His grace is poured out on you for the benefit of others. Your innermost parts are like a field of wheat, sprouting to feed the hungry. All of this is surrounded with the lilies of your purity.

CHAPTER 7:3—*Your two breasts are like two young fawns that are twins.*

What would happen if the bride of Christ were able to bear children but could not nourish them? The Bridegroom shows that His bride is not only a mother but a nurse. You have abundant nourishment for all who need it. His grace continually flows out through you as the need arises. You would have nothing to give unless you were completely united to Him. Through your union with Him you receive all the grace that you give to others.

CHAPTER 7:4—*Your neck is a tower of ivory; your eyes like the fish pools of Hebron, which are in the gate of the daughter of the multitude; your nose is as the tower of Lebanon, which looks toward Damascus.*

The neck represents strength. God makes you pure and strong like ivory. The strength of God within you is a tower where you hide from every danger. You run into Him as you see your enemies approach. This spiritual foresight is symbolized by the eyes. As you see with the insight of God, your eyes become like fish pools (a source of blessing and a remedy for every ill). God keeps the mind that has willingly been given up to him. He makes use of it, in a thousand ways, for the good of everyone He wants to help.

The fish pools are at the gate of the "daughter of the multitude." This "daughter" is the imagination, which disturbs the clarity of the mind. Your imagination will try and distract you from the deep fellowship you can have with God's Spirit. But this point in the journey is a place where you are no longer distracted by the multitude of silly and annoying thoughts. God has set up a door between your spirit and your soul. You have learned to retreat to your spirit and close the door behind you, there to enjoy uninterrupted fellowship with God.

101

The nose is the symbol of sound judgment. Here, the nose has become like the tower of Lebanon—strong and unable to be turned aside. You have lost your own way of judging and reasoning to inherit the prudence of God. Each moment is spent beholding God, and no action is taken unless it is seen in God. You walk from moment to moment beholding your God in faith. The ways of God outshine the ways of man.

CHAPTER 7:5—*Your head is like Mount Carmel; the hair of your head is like the purple of the King bound by the water courses.*

The head is like a mountain elevated in God. The hair represents all the gifts with which you have been favored. These gifts are from God and belong entirely to God. You can make no claim on them. All good that you possess belongs to Him. The head is adorned with decorations of the King's royal purple. Grace is brought by way of the water course—it flows directly from God, and directly back to God. There is free passage between you and God for you neither resist nor hinder His blessings.

CHAPTER 7:6—*How fair and how pleasant you are, my love, for delights!*

God sees a reflection of Himself in His beloved. She is His delight, just as He is the delight of the Father. In being His perfect mirror, the bride brings the Bridegroom quiet pleasure. She is fair and enchanting, for she is clothed with His perfection. She is His delight, and He is hers.

Chapter 7:7—*Your stature is like a palm tree, and your breasts are like clusters of grapes.*

Your stature, the state of your spiritual life, is like an upright palm tree. The blessings which God gives do not turn you toward your own interests. Note that the beautiful palm tree has two unique characteristics. The more fruit the tree bears, the straighter it becomes. Also the palm tree will not bear fruit unless it falls under the shadow of a male palm.

In the same way, the bride has two unique characteristics: She never uses for herself the grace that God gives her, and she lives under the shadow of the Bridegroom. This causes her to act with perfect timing in the perfect season.

The breasts of His bride are like clusters of grapes. The grape, though full of sweetness, retains none for itself. The grape yields all that it is to the wine presser. So, likewise, the more you are cast down and persecuted, the more kindly you will act to those that treat you with evil intent.

CHAPTER 7:8—*I said, I will go up to the palm-tree, and I will take hold of the fruit of it; your breasts shall be as clusters of the vine, and the smell of your mouth like that of apples.*

A young daughter, who has heard the praises of the King from His beloved, longs to learn from this wise woman. This young believer wants to reap the fruit that comes from the annointing that rests upon His bride. Her words are like a sweet cluster of grapes; her pure teachings bring forth a wonderful fragrance.

CHAPTER 7:9—*Your throat, like the best wine, is fit for my beloved to drink, and to be dwelt upon with delight by his lips and teeth.*

The young daughter of Zion continues to praise the bride. The throat is the inward part of the spirit through which flows the wine of God. His presence is perfectly fluid and flows between the spirit of the believer and Himself.[1] This wine is for God's drinking: His Spirit flows back and forth between Himself and His bride. He changes and transforms her with pleasure and delight. He forms and reforms her—causing her to diminish so that she might reappear wholly transformed in Him. How wonderful and how worthy to be the drink of God! Here is the highest good and the final end of the believer.

CHAPTER 7:10—*I am my beloved's and his desire is toward me.*

You hear the truth spoken of by the young daughter of Zion and confess it to be true. The passionate love of your Beloved has consumed you.

You are so lost in Him that you can never find yourself. Now, more than ever before, you are your Beloved's. He has transformed you into His likeness. He will never cast you away, and you no longer fear any separation from Him. God will never banish you from His presence. You are confirmed in love forever. Love has had its perfect work within you. The Beloved sees nothing in you that is not absolutely of and for Him. He cannot turn away His desire nor His gaze from you.

CHAPTER 7:11—*Come, my beloved, let us go forth into the field; let us lodge in the villages.*

The beloved of the Lord no longer fears anything. You see Him in all circumstances. You have begun to explore the immense freedom of God Himself. Of course you have not become God, but you have come into a union of love with Him. He flows through you perfectly.

No longer do you fear losing Him for you are deeply united with Him. You invite Him to go forth from the enclosure of the garden and the chambers. There is now no place too small or too large for you, since your place is in God Himself. The bride wants to go forth with her Beloved to win many others to Him.

CHAPTER 7:12—*Let us get up early to the vineyards; let us see if the vine flourishes, if the flowers bring forth fruit, and the pomegranate blossoms; there I will give you my breasts.*

You now invite your Bridegroom to go everywhere. You are full of activity. As God acts without while He rests within, so it is with you. Whatever action you did before from your own strength, you now do perfectly in His strength.[2]

You are no longer concerned with your own ends or your accomplishments—everything is to and through your God. In the church you see thousands of things to be accomplished for the Bridegroom's glory. These works you accomplish through His strength and providence.

But, dear bride, explain yourself. What do you mean by saying that *you will give* your breasts to the Bridegroom? He is the One that causes them to be fruitful! If, however, in your perfect liberty you no longer have any selfish motivation for serving God, you do indeed give the Beloved all of your good works and all of your devotion. Everything you do is toward Him. He is your beginning and your end.

CHAPTER 7:13—*The mandrakes give off a pleasant fragrance, and at our gates are all manner of pleasant fruits, new and old, which I have laid up for you, my beloved.*

All things are common between the Bridegroom and His beloved. You have nothing that belongs to

106

yourself; your possessions are also His. You no longer have any property or interests of your own. All you do is a fruitful offering to your Lord. You give Him both the old works which He worked in you from the beginning and the new works which He accomplishes in you from moment to moment. Everything has been surrendered to Him. All that you are is entirely for the King's use.

Notes To Chapter Seven

1. Pour a fluid into a vessel and you will see it rest, quietly bounded by the lines that limit the vase, and assuming perfectly its exact shape. It has no form or figure of its own, but only that of the vessel in which it is contained.

   Such, however, is not the natural pliancy of the soul. It has its own set form and sharp outline, due to its habits and inclinations, and its will in self. And when a person refuses to come forth from these we say that he is hard, that is, obstinate and willful. *I will take the stony heart out of their flesh,* saith the Lord God (*Ez.* 11:19), that is, I will take away their stiffneckedness.

   Wood, iron, and stone must feel the wedge, the hammer and the fire before they will change their form; and so must it be with a heart that resembles them in its hardness and insusceptibility to divine impressions, and remains entrenched in its own will and fortified by the inclinations which follow in the train of our corrupted nature. A heart on the other hand that is plastic, soft and yielding, is called a melted or liquified heart.—*The Love of God,* by St. Francis of Sales.

2. It would have been a serious defect in the bride, if, when she should have remained entirely passive she had chosen to act, for in this way she would have hindered the operations of God; she would have been acting from her own activity, when God required her to be perfectly passive, that she might die to all self-originated influences. Now, through her continued passivity, she has become like soft wax, or a perfectly manageable instrument in the hands of God, with which He does as He will. She has then reached the only true passivity in its perfection, an active-passive state, in which her actions are no longer self-originated, but are wholly due to the gentle and loving influences of the Holy Spirit within.—*Justifications.*

8

CHAPTER 8:1—*Oh, that you were like a brother to me, who nursed at my mother's breast. If I found you outdoors I would kiss you. No one would despise me, either.*

You desire to know your Bridegroom in still a deeper way. Although you enjoy permanent and enduring communion with your Beloved, you must go here and there and busy yourself with the concerns of the household. Yet there are times when the Bridegroom and the bride want to embrace each other more completely. Such closeness is what you now desire. Who will give you the divine Husband? Your Husband is also your brother because you both have the same Father. Hidden with Him in God, you draw nourishment with Him and through Him, by means of the Father who is the source of all things.

But now you want to experience Him outwardly as much as you do inwardly. The inward is changed much earlier than the outward. For awhile certain external flaws, which hide the abundance of inner grace, do not displease the Bridegroom. Yet, these outer weaknesses are still flaws and they bring a certain shame with them. Now you cry out for your Beloved to transform your outward appearance. This is not requested for your own vanity, but for the glory of God.

CHAPTER 8:2—*I will lay hold of you and bring you into my mother's house. There you will teach me and I will give you a bowl of spiced wine, the new wine of my pomegranates.*

Your spirit experiences two things as it enjoys fellowship with God. One, you find that you are in God just like an empty vase, thrown in the ocean, is full of the water and surrounded by the water at the same time. You hold Him and are held by Him at the same time. And where do you hold Him? In the only place you can go—into the bosom of the Father, the place of your birth (i.e. your mother's house).

The other thing you experience is His instruction as He teaches you the special things which are only shared with His bride. He tells you all you need to know and reveals to you the unsurpassed love of the Father. This is all taught with little fanfare: It is whispered in the unspeakable but eloquent silence of God. The Word unceasingly speaks to your spirit and teaches you in a way that surpasses the best human teachers.

But as He teaches you more and more, you allow Him to drink deeper and deeper of your "spiced wine." This is your gift which you forever offer up before Him in great purity. There is a constant stream of love flowing back and forth between you and your Beloved. You partake of the fellowship of God, for you give back to Him all that you receive.

CHAPTER 8:3—*His left hand should be under my head, and his right hand should embrace me.*

God has two arms with which He holds and embraces you. One is His all-powerful protection, and the other is His perfect love. This holy embrace is simply the enjoyment and union you have with God. When you say that His hand should embrace you, you are not talking about something that has not already happened. You have experienced this already, but you look forward to eternity and see how it will be forever.

CHAPTER 8:4—*I charge you, daughters of Jerusalem, that you do not stir up, nor awaken my love, until she please.*

This is the third time that the Bridegroom asks that His beloved be not awakened from her sleep. There are many different kinds of inward sleep. One may detach you from your entanglements with the world. Another is a sleep of death where you die in the arms of your Beloved. You cannot be called forth until it is time for your spiritual resurrection. Still another kind is the sleep of rest in God. Here is permanent and lasting rest: a rest that is calm, sweet, and enduring. This rest shall never be disturbed.

Now the Bridegroom wants to teach His bride that only complete self-complacency and contempt of others could cause her to depart from Him. In the next verse He shows you what He has saved you from, the corruptness of your old nature. He does this so you will never lose sight of your humility.

CHAPTER 8:5—*Who is this that comes up from the wilderness, complete with delights, leaning on the arm of her beloved? I raised you up under the appletree. There your mother was corrupted, and there you were conceived.*

Gradually you have come up from the desert since you left it. The desert is not only that desert of pure faith, but also the desert of self. You are delighted because you are like a pitcher filled to the brim, with spring water spilling over the sides. No longer are you self-supported. No longer do you fear the abundance of these delights. You do not fear being overthrown, for you walk leaning on the strength of your Beloved. What gain it is to lose all external support in order to lean only on your Beloved!

"I raised you up under the appletree." God awakens you from the sleep of death and raises you up into a new life. He saves you from the corrupt and spoiled nature which came to you by birth.

God's work aims at accomplishing two things: delivering you from your fallen nature and restoring you to God in fullness. In her innocence Eve belonged to God completely, but she withdrew from God to unite with the Devil and his plan—and all of us have been affected by the results.

You are born into the world like an illegitimate child who has no idea who his father is. But God comes and draws you out of your old life. He cleanses you and gives you back your innocence. He is the One who raises you up from under the apple tree where you lived in sin.

CHAPTER 8:6—*Set me as a seal upon your heart, as a seal upon your arm; for love is as strong as death; jealousy is as cruel as the grave. The light it produces is the light of intense fire and flames.*

You desire your Bridegroom to set Himself as a seal upon your heart. He is the source of your life. He is the one who stops you from leaving your blessed dwelling place. You are a fountain sealed unto Christ.

Let everything be unto Him. Do nothing without His direction. You are an enclosed garden for your Bridegroom. What He shuts, no man can open; and what He opens, no man can shut. "For love is as strong as death," and He will do what He pleases with you. He causes you to die so that you will live by Him alone. "Jealousy is as cruel as the grave"— that is why He encloses you so completely. The lamps are lamps of fire which enlighten while they burn, and consume while giving light.

CHAPTER 8:7—*Many waters cannot quench love, nor can the floods drown it; if a man would give all the substance of his house for love, it would be utterly condemned.*

The many waters of trials, setbacks, uncertainties, poverty, and distress are not able to quench your love for God. Therefore, do not think that trusting Him completely will dampen your love for Him.

If you have courage enough to give everything that you are to God, then do not think that after you have made so worthy a move you will somehow regret it. This simply will not be possible once you know the freedom that abandonment to God brings. God will show you how completely difficult it is for you to leave Him after you have tasted of Him deeply.

CHAPTER 8:8—*We have a little sister and she has no breasts; what shall we do for our sister in the day when she shall be spoken for?*

How glorious to share all things in common with your Bridegroom. You discuss with Him the affairs of others and talk with Him about household matters. "What shall we do with the little sister who is still tender and pure but unprepared for deep communion with You? She is not ready for the deep things of God, nor is she ready to help others." Here is how the bride should consult her Beloved on behalf of others.

CHAPTER 8:9—*If she were a wall, we could build upon it bulwarks of silver; if she were a door, we could frame it with boards of cedar.*

The Lord replies, "If she already knows surrender of her own will to Me and also has confidence in Me, we will begin to build on that foundation; and we will build bulwarks of silver. This will defend her against those who try to dissuade her from an inward walk—especially from human reason and subtle aspects of self-love. But if she has just come through the door, just beginning to learn the life in Christ, we will build her up with grace; we will frame her with graces and characteristics which will have the beauty and strength of cedar.

CHAPTER 8:10—*I am a wall, and my breasts like towers; then was I in his eyes as one that found favor.*

You have heard the wonderful plan of your Beloved. You see how successful His plan has been carried out in you. You, yourself, have become a wall of strength: a place of protection to others.

You know you will never be lost, for He has showered His favor upon you.

CHAPTER 8:11—*The Peaceable One (Solomon) has a vineyard, which has people in it (Baal-Hamon); he has delivered it to keepers; each one brings for the fruit a thousand pieces of silver.*

God takes pleasure in putting to rest all doubts. Someone might think that because you no longer possess yourself, and because you perform no more outstanding works, you do not matter to God's kingdom. God is a God of peace. God has a vineyard whose care He has given to His bride, and yet all the members that make up His bride *are* that vineyard. God made His spouse very fruitful, and then He commissioned His angels to watch over her. These are the keepers of the vineyard. It is a profitable vineyard, both for God and for the bride. He gives her the privilege of partaking of the fruits, and she will never lose this position she is now in.

CHAPTER 8:12—*My vineyard is before me; You, Peaceable Lord, must have a thousand pieces of silver for it; and those that maintain the fruit of your vineyard will have two hundred pieces.*

You are not slack concerning the care of the vineyard. You give everything to nurturing it. All things that are done in God are done with a wonderful ease and freedom. You watch and cultivate the vineyard, but it is all for the Bridegroom. Perfect love does not know what it is to consider self-interest.

CHAPTER 8:13—*You that dwell in the garden, your companions in the garden hear your voice; let me hear it, too.*

The Bridegroom invites you to speak on His behalf and to teach others of Him. He asks you to leave the beauty of His garden, for your companions are calling for you. He asks of you something new: to leave the profound silence in which you have dwelled. During your whole faith experience you remained in great silence so that God might reduce you to simplicity and unite you completely with Himself. Now He desires that you go forth, though in the unutterable and rich silence of your inward spirit. He desires that the one would not interfere with the other.

God desires a harmony between the silence of the spirit and the outward speech and actions of the body. Spirit, soul, and body should all be united in their praise to God. Praise of the lips is not enough if the heart does not agree. Neither one is sufficient if the praise does not originate in the spirit. When all three are in perfect harmony, there is true adoration of your Beloved.

But once you have grown accustomed to dwelling in that deep and wonderful silence of God, then you will try to preserve it. You are somewhat afraid of interrupting it. The Lord will come and try to rid you of this tendency by calling you out of your silent comfort! "Let me hear your voice," He asks. It is time to learn to praise Me in a more outward way. You have already done so in admirable silence. Besides inward and unspeakable praise, God wants to give you a facility of speech in talking with Him.

He also invites you to talk to others of inward things. He wants to teach you about what pleases Him. One of the first duties of the bride is to teach others to love Him perfectly and inwardly. This is what the Bridegroom desires of His bride: to address Him both with silence and with voice.

Chapter 8:14—*Flee away, my beloved, and be like a gazelle or a young deer on the mountains of spices.*

When you have lost all self-interest, you beg Him to turn away lest He should see something that displeases Him.[1] May He leave the place which offers Him no sweet fragrance; let Him come to the ones who are like mountains of spices. These are the ones who get their lovely fragrance from Him.

When you arrive at this point you care only for the interests of your Beloved.[2] You forever labor for your Lord; you endure rebuke and persecution. No thought is for your own success. You cannot bear that your God would be dishonored or displeased.

This does not mean that you are always looking to enjoy the sweet presence of God. By no means! You allow Him to come and go as He pleases. You no longer expect distinct seasons when you consciously enjoy His presence. Here is evidence that you dwell in your spirit. You continually rejoice at the wonderful plan of your Beloved. You love Him to go where He pleases, to visit other hearts and win them over.[3]

Let Him delight in the spiced ones who have come to Him! As for you, what He does with you is entirely up to His wisdom. Death and life are equally acceptable to you, for your love is incomparably stronger than before. This is the fruit of the work of the Lord.

Notes To Chapter Eight

1. It seems to me very easy to understand that one who places his happiness in God alone can no longer desire his own felicity. None but he who dwells in God by love can place all his happiness in God alone; and when a Christian is thus disposed, he desires no other felicity than that of God in Himself and for Himself; and thus no enjoyment with an end of self, not even the glory of heaven, can be a source of satisfaction, nor consequently an object of desire. Desire is ever the child of Love; if my love be in God alone and for Himself alone, without respect to self, my desires will be in Him alone, and equally pure of selfish motive.

   This desire in God no longer presents the vivacity of the former desire of love, resulting from an absence of the thing desired; it has the quietness and repose of a desire completely filled and satisfied. For God being infinitely perfect and forever blessed, and the happiness of the believer consisting in this perfection and blessedness of God, his desires cannot manifest the restlessness of unsatisfied wants, but must present the repose of one who has no ungratified wish. This, then, is the foundation of the believer's state, and this is the reason that he does not perceive in himself all the good desires of those who still love God from a regard to self, nor of those who love and seek self in the affection which they manifest for God.

   It must not be supposed, however, that God cannot implant such dispositions and desires in the believer's heart as may seem good to Himself. Thus He sometimes causes him to feel the weight of his tabernacle and to exclaim: *I am in a strait betwixt two, desiring to depart and to be with Christ which is far better* (Phil. 1:23). And at another time, under the constraining influence of love for the brethren, and of an absolute freedom from every selfish consideration, he might cry out: *I could wish that myself were accursed from Christ for my brethren* (Rom. 9:3). These apparently contradictory feelings are perfectly reconciled in the depths of the spirit. The totally abandoned Christian does not have

120

desires like those of the former days, which had their seat in the selfish will, but they are stirred up and excited by God Himself, without any thought on the part of the self. He holds the heart so immovably turned towards Himself, that He is the author of its desires as well as of all its other acts, without any aid from the soul. A desire having reference to self is the necessary result of a will still unpurified from self; but as the whole design of God is to destroy the will of the self-nature by making the Christian's will one with His own, so He must at the same time necessarily absorb and destroy every self-originated desire.

There is still another reason why God takes away and implants desires at His own good pleasure. Designing to confer some blessing upon his follower, He first infuses a desire in the follower's heart for the particular blessing He Himself wants to give, in order that He may hear and grant the request. *Lord, Thou hast heard the desire of the humble; Thou wilt prepare their heart, Thou wilt cause thine ear to hear,* (Psalm 10:17). He prepares the heart and grants the request. *Delight thyself also in the Lord and He shall give thee the desires of thine heart,* (Psalm 37:4). The Spirit making intercession in and for the believer, then the believer's desires and requests are those of the Holy Ghost, (Rom. 8:26), and Jesus Christ dwelling in him declares, *I know that Thou hearest me always,* (John 11:42).

At other times He inclines the Christian to pray for particular things, and the Christian is perfectly conscious that the prayer is not originated in his own will, but in the will of God; for he is not free to pray for whom he pleases, nor when he pleases, but when he prays his requests are always heard and granted. This produces no self-gratulation in it; the believer is perfectly aware that it is He who possesses him, that prays and grants His own petitions. All this seems to me infinitely clearer in my own mind that I can make it in words.—*Justifications.*

2. To bless God and to thank Him for every event of his providence is, in truth, a great attainment in holiness. But while we leave to God alone the care of willing and doing in

us, by us and through us, just what He pleases, without any solicitude as to what is going on, though we perceive it distinctly—if we can at the same time occupy our hearts and fix our attention upon the divine gentleness and goodness, adoring Him with thanksgiving, not in effects or in the events He ordains, but in Himself and in His own infinite excellence, we shall be engaged in a far higher and more blessed employment.

The daughter of a skillful physician lay in a continued fever, and knowing the deep attachment and singular love her father had for her, she said to one of her young friends: I feel a great deal of pain, but the thought of a remedy for it never crosses my mind, for I know nothing of their curative virtues. I might desire one thing when quite another was what I required. Do I not do well, then, to leave the whole care of that matter to my father, who does know, and who can and will do for me whatever is necessary for my recovery? I should do wrong to think about it, for he will think for me; I should do wrong to wish for anything, for he will see that I have everything that is good for me. I will wait, and let him will whatever he thinks best; my only occupation shall be to look to him, to testify my filial love for him, and to manifest my implicit confidence in his love. Her father asked her if she did not desire to be bled, in order to recover? I am thine, my father, she replied; I know not what I ought to desire in order to get well; thou must both will and do for me of thy good pleasure; as for me, it is enough for me to love and honor thee with all my heart, as I do. Behold now her arm bandaged, and her father opening the vein with his lancet; but while he cuts and the blood flows, his daughter never turns her eyes from her father's face, to behold her bleeding arm, but keeps them fixed upon his countenance with a look of affection, saying nothing except an occasional expression, "My father loves me, and I am wholly his." When all was over, she did not thank him, but only repeated the same expressions of her attachment and filial confidence.—*The Love of God,* by St. Francis of Sales.

3. The greater the purity and simplicity of a substance, the more extended is its usefulness. Nothing can be purer or simpler than water, and what a vast range of uses does it present on account of its fluidity! It is ready to receive all sorts of impressions with facility. Tasteless in itself, it may be infinitely varied in flavor; colorless, it becomes susceptible of every color in turn. Thus it is with the believer's spirit and will, in a state of simplicity and purity; having neither flavor nor color derived from self, God is the author of whatever of either they may manifest, just as the water owes its scent or its hue to the will of him who prepared it. It is not correct, however, to say that the water, however flavored or however colored, is in itself possessed of these qualities, inasmuch as they are but accidental and impressed upon it from without, and it is its very quality of freedom from taste and color that enables it to exhibit every variety of both. I feel this to be the state of my inmost being; it can no longer distinguish or take knowledge of anything in itself or as belonging to itself, and this constitutes its purity; but it receives everything bestowed upon it, just as it comes, without holding any part of it as for itself.

Should you ask of this water, what are its properties, it would reply that its property is to have none at all. But, you may reply, I have seen you of a red color; I dare say, it would answer, "But I am not, for all that, red. I am not so by nature, nor do I reflect upon what is done with me either in imparting to me flavor or color."

It is the same with form as with color. As water is fluid and yielding, it instantly and exactly assumes the form of the vessel in which it is placed.—Had it consistence and properties of its own, it could not thus take every form, receive every taste, exhibit every flavor and appear of every hue.—*Justifications,* by Jeanne Guyon.

PLEASE CALL FOR CURRENT PRICES

CHURCH LIFE
An Open Letter to House Church Leaders (Edwards)
When the Church Was Led Only By Laymen (Edwards)
Beyond Radical (Edwards)
How to Meet Under the Headship of Jesus Christ (Edwards)
The Open Church (Rutz)
Revolution, The Story of the Early Church (Edwards)
Church Unity (Litzman, Nee, Edwards)
Let's Return to Church Unity (Kurosaki)
Climb the Highest Mountain (Edwards)
The Torch of the Testimony (Kennedy)
Passing of the Torch (Chen)
Going to Church in the First Century (Banks)
When the Church Was Young (Loosley)
The Silas Diary (Edwards)
Rethinking Elders (Edwards)

ON THE DEEPER CHRISTIAN LIFE
The Highest Life (Edwards)
The Secret to the Christian Life (Edwards)
Bone of His Bone (Huegel)
The Centrality of Jesus Christ (T. Austin-Sparks)
The House of God (T. Austin-Sparks)
The Ultimate Intention (Fromke)
Final Steps in Christian Maturity (Guyon)

LIBRARY OF SPIRITUAL CLASSICS
Practicing His Presence (Lawrence/Laubach)
Experiencing the Depths of Jesus Christ (Guyon)
Union With God (Guyon)
The Seeking Heart (Fenelon)
The Spiritual Guide (Molinos)
The Song of the Bride (Guyon)

SEEDSOWERS PUBLISHING HOUSE
800-645-2342